Competitive Threats
Complete Self-Assessment Guide

The guidance in this Self-Assessment is base⌐
best practices and standards in business process architecture, design
and quality management. The guidance is also based on the professional
judgment of the individual collaborators listed in the Acknowledgments.

Notice of rights

Trademarks

Table of Contents

About The Art of Service

The Art of Service, Business Process Architects since 2000, is dedicated to helping stakeholders achieve excellence.

Defining, designing, creating, and implementing a process to solve a stakeholders challenge or meet an objective is the most valuable role... In EVERY group, company, organization and department.

Unless you're talking a one-time, single-use project, there should be a process. Whether that process is managed and implemented by humans, AI, or a combination of the two, it needs to be designed by someone with a complex enough perspective to ask the right questions.

Someone capable of asking the right questions and step back and say, 'What are we really trying to accomplish here? And is there a different way to look at it?'

With The Art of Service's Standard Requirements Self-Assessments, we empower people who can do just that — whether their title is marketer, entrepreneur, manager, salesperson, consultant, Business Process Manager, executive assistant, IT Manager, CIO etc... —they are the people who rule the future. They are people who watch the process as it happens, and ask the right questions to make the process work better.

Contact us when you need any support with this Self-Assessment and any help with templates, blue-prints and examples of standard documents you might need:

http://theartofservice.com
service@theartofservice.com

Included Resources - how to access

Included with your purchase of the book is the Competitive

Threats Self-Assessment Spreadsheet Dashboard which contains all questions and Self-Assessment areas and auto-generates insights, graphs, and project RACI planning - all with examples to get you started right away.

How? Simply send an email to
access@theartofservice.com
with this books' title in the subject to get the
Competitive Threats Self Assessment Tool right away.

You will receive the following contents with New and Updated specific criteria:

- The latest quick edition of the book in PDF

- The latest complete edition of the book in PDF, which criteria correspond to the criteria in...

- The Self-Assessment Excel Dashboard, and...

- Example pre-filled Self-Assessment Excel Dashboard to get familiar with results generation

- In-depth specific Checklists covering the topic

- Project management checklists and templates to assist with implementation

INCLUDES LIFETIME SELF ASSESSMENT UPDATES

Every self assessment comes with Lifetime Updates and Lifetime Free Updated Books. Lifetime Updates is an industry-first feature which allows you to receive verified self assessment updates, ensuring you always have the most accurate information at your fingertips.

Get it now- you will be glad you did - do it now, before you forget.

Send an email to **access@theartofservice.com** with this books' title in the subject to get the Competitive Threats Self Assessment Tool right away.

Purpose of this Self-Assessment

This Self-Assessment has been developed to improve understanding of the requirements and elements of Competitive Threats, based on best practices and standards in business process architecture, design and quality management.

It is designed to allow for a rapid Self-Assessment to determine how closely existing management practices and procedures correspond to the elements of the Self-Assessment.

The criteria of requirements and elements of Competitive Threats have been rephrased in the format of a Self-Assessment questionnaire, with a seven-criterion scoring system, as explained in this document.

In this format, even with limited background knowledge of Competitive Threats, a manager can quickly review existing operations to determine how they measure up to the standards. This in turn can serve as the starting point of a 'gap analysis' to identify management tools or system elements that might usefully be implemented in the organization to help improve overall performance.

How to use the Self-Assessment

On the following pages are a series of questions to identify to what extent your Competitive Threats initiative is complete in comparison to the requirements set in standards.

To facilitate answering the questions, there is a space in front of each question to enter a score on a scale of '1' to '5'.

1 Strongly Disagree

2 Disagree

3 Neutral

4 Agree

5 Strongly Agree

Read the question and rate it with the following in front of mind:

'In my belief,
the answer to this question is clearly defined'.

There are two ways in which you can choose to interpret this statement;
1. how aware are you that the answer to the question is clearly defined
2. for more in-depth analysis you can choose to gather evidence and confirm the answer to the question. This obviously will take more time, most Self-Assessment users opt for the first way to interpret the question and dig deeper later on based on the outcome of the overall Self-Assessment.

A score of '1' would mean that the answer is not clear at all, where a '5' would mean the answer is crystal clear and defined. Leave emtpy when the question is not applicable or you don't want to answer it, you can skip it without affecting your score. Write your score in the space provided.

After you have responded to all the appropriate statements in each section, compute your average score for that section, using the formula provided, and round to the nearest tenth. Then transfer to the corresponding spoke in the Competitive Threats Scorecard on the second next page of the Self-Assessment.

Your completed Competitive Threats Scorecard will give you a clear presentation of which Competitive Threats areas need attention.

Competitive Threats Scorecard Example

Example of how the finalized Scorecard can look like:

Competitive Threats Scorecard

Your Scores:

BEGINNING OF THE SELF-ASSESSMENT:

CRITERION #1: RECOGNIZE

INTENT: Be aware of the need for change. Recognize that there is an unfavorable variation, problem or symptom.

In my belief, the answer to this question is clearly defined:

5 Strongly Agree

4 Agree

3 Neutral

2 Disagree

1 Strongly Disagree

1. Looking at each person individually – does every one have the qualities which are needed to work in this group?
<--- Score

2. What training and capacity building actions are needed to implement proposed reforms?
<--- Score

3. What are the competitive threats resources needed?
<--- Score

4. How do you assess your competitive threats workforce capability and capacity needs, including skills, competencies, and staffing levels?
<--- Score

5. How are training requirements identified?
<--- Score

6. Which information does the competitive threats business case need to include?
<--- Score

7. Who needs budgets?
<--- Score

8. Does your organization need more competitive threats education?
<--- Score

9. Are there any revenue recognition issues?
<--- Score

10. Is it needed?
<--- Score

11. What creative shifts do you need to take?
<--- Score

12. Think about the people you identified for your competitive threats project and the project responsibilities you would assign to them, what kind of training do you think they would need to perform these responsibilities effectively?

<--- Score

13. What situation(s) led to this competitive threats Self Assessment?
<--- Score

14. What does competitive threats success mean to the stakeholders?
<--- Score

15. What else needs to be measured?
<--- Score

16. Is the quality assurance team identified?
<--- Score

17. Does competitive threats create potential expectations in other areas that need to be recognized and considered?
<--- Score

18. Who defines the rules in relation to any given issue?
<--- Score

19. Who should resolve the competitive threats issues?
<--- Score

20. To what extent does each concerned units management team recognize competitive threats as an effective investment?
<--- Score

21. Who else hopes to benefit from it?
<--- Score

22. What activities does the governance board need to consider?
<--- Score

23. What are the minority interests and what amount of minority interests can be recognized?
<--- Score

24. What would happen if competitive threats weren't done?
<--- Score

25. How does it fit into your organizational needs and tasks?
<--- Score

26. Where do you need to exercise leadership?
<--- Score

27. How do you recognize an competitive threats objection?
<--- Score

28. What is the recognized need?
<--- Score

29. What are the clients issues and concerns?
<--- Score

30. Did you miss any major competitive threats issues?
<--- Score

31. Who needs what information?
<--- Score

32. How do you identify the kinds of information that you will need?
<--- Score

33. Do you know what you need to know about competitive threats?
<--- Score

34. Are there recognized competitive threats problems?
<--- Score

35. Do you need to avoid or amend any competitive threats activities?
<--- Score

36. Consider your own competitive threats project, what types of organizational problems do you think might be causing or affecting your problem, based on the work done so far?
<--- Score

37. What is the smallest subset of the problem you can usefully solve?
<--- Score

38. For your competitive threats project, identify and describe the business environment, is there more than one layer to the business environment?
<--- Score

39. What problems are you facing and how do you consider competitive threats will circumvent those obstacles?
<--- Score

40. Will competitive threats deliverables need to be tested and, if so, by whom?
<--- Score

41. Why the need?
<--- Score

42. What resources or support might you need?
<--- Score

43. Are there regulatory / compliance issues?
<--- Score

44. What is the problem or issue?
<--- Score

45. What are your needs in relation to competitive threats skills, labor, equipment, and markets?
<--- Score

46. Are you dealing with any of the same issues today as yesterday? What can you do about this?
<--- Score

47. Is the need for organizational change recognized?
<--- Score

48. Who are your key stakeholders who need to sign off?
<--- Score

49. Is it clear when you think of the day ahead of you what activities and tasks you need to complete?
<--- Score

50. As a sponsor, customer or management, how important is it to meet goals, objectives?
<--- Score

51. What needs to be done?
<--- Score

52. Do you recognize competitive threats achievements?
<--- Score

53. How do you take a forward-looking perspective in identifying competitive threats research related to market response and models?
<--- Score

54. When a competitive threats manager recognizes a problem, what options are available?
<--- Score

55. Which issues are too important to ignore?
<--- Score

56. Have you identified your competitive threats key performance indicators?
<--- Score

57. Are controls defined to recognize and contain problems?
<--- Score

58. What needs to stay?
<--- Score

59. What prevents you from making the changes you know will make you a more effective

competitive threats leader?
<--- Score

60. What are the timeframes required to resolve each of the issues/problems?
<--- Score

61. What are the expected benefits of competitive threats to the stakeholder?
<--- Score

62. How many trainings, in total, are needed?
<--- Score

63. What should be considered when identifying available resources, constraints, and deadlines?
<--- Score

64. What is the competitive threats problem definition? What do you need to resolve?
<--- Score

65. Are employees recognized or rewarded for performance that demonstrates the highest levels of integrity?
<--- Score

66. How much are sponsors, customers, partners, stakeholders involved in competitive threats? In other words, what are the risks, if competitive threats does not deliver successfully?
<--- Score

67. What is the extent or complexity of the competitive threats problem?
<--- Score

68. What do employees need in the short term?
<--- Score

69. Will it solve real problems?
<--- Score

70. Why is this needed?
<--- Score

71. Are problem definition and motivation clearly presented?
<--- Score

72. To what extent would your organization benefit from being recognized as a award recipient?
<--- Score

73. What competitive threats events should you attend?
<--- Score

74. Who needs to know?
<--- Score

75. Whom do you really need or want to serve?
<--- Score

76. Which needs are not included or involved?
<--- Score

77. What tools and technologies are needed for a custom competitive threats project?
<--- Score

78. How are you going to measure success?
<--- Score

79. What competitive threats capabilities do you need?
<--- Score

80. Will new equipment/products be required to facilitate competitive threats delivery, for example is new software needed?
<--- Score

81. What information do users need?
<--- Score

82. Are there competitive threats problems defined?
<--- Score

83. How can auditing be a preventative security measure?
<--- Score

84. How do you identify subcontractor relationships?
<--- Score

85. Does the problem have ethical dimensions?
<--- Score

86. Where is training needed?
<--- Score

87. Can management personnel recognize the monetary benefit of competitive threats?
<--- Score

88. Are employees recognized for desired behaviors?
<--- Score

89. What are the stakeholder objectives to be achieved with competitive threats?
<--- Score

90. Do you have/need 24-hour access to key personnel?
<--- Score

91. Are your goals realistic? Do you need to redefine your problem? Perhaps the problem has changed or maybe you have reached your goal and need to set a new one?
<--- Score

92. How are the competitive threats's objectives aligned to the group's overall stakeholder strategy?
<--- Score

93. Are there any specific expectations or concerns about the competitive threats team, competitive threats itself?
<--- Score

94. Who needs to know about competitive threats?
<--- Score

95. What is the problem and/or vulnerability?
<--- Score

96. What competitive threats coordination do you need?
<--- Score

97. What vendors make products that address the competitive threats needs?
<--- Score

98. Will a response program recognize when a crisis occurs and provide some level of response?
<--- Score

99. Would you recognize a threat from the inside?
<--- Score

Add up total points for this section:
_____ = Total points for this section

Divided by: _____ (number of statements answered) = _____
Average score for this section

Transfer your score to the competitive threats Index at the beginning of the Self-Assessment.

CRITERION #2: DEFINE:

INTENT: Formulate the stakeholder problem. Define the problem, needs and objectives.

In my belief, the answer to this question is clearly defined:

5 Strongly Agree

4 Agree

3 Neutral

2 Disagree

1 Strongly Disagree

1. Is there a completed SIPOC representation, describing the Suppliers, Inputs, Process, Outputs, and Customers?
<--- Score

2. How does the competitive threats manager ensure against scope creep?
<--- Score

3. Have the customer needs been translated into specific, measurable requirements? How?
<--- Score

4. What scope do you want your strategy to cover?
<--- Score

5. Are resources adequate for the scope?
<--- Score

6. What are the boundaries of the scope? What is in bounds and what is not? What is the start point? What is the stop point?
<--- Score

7. What is the scope of competitive threats?
<--- Score

8. What constraints exist that might impact the team?
<--- Score

9. Is special competitive threats user knowledge required?
<--- Score

10. Is there a completed, verified, and validated high-level 'as is' (not 'should be' or 'could be') stakeholder process map?
<--- Score

11. How do you gather requirements?
<--- Score

12. How often are the team meetings?
<--- Score

13. Does the scope remain the same?
<--- Score

14. Are task requirements clearly defined?
<--- Score

15. What information should you gather?
<--- Score

16. What are the tasks and definitions?
<--- Score

17. When are meeting minutes sent out? Who is on the distribution list?
<--- Score

18. Have specific policy objectives been defined?
<--- Score

19. Are accountability and ownership for competitive threats clearly defined?
<--- Score

20. Is the competitive threats scope manageable?
<--- Score

21. Do you all define competitive threats in the same way?
<--- Score

22. Is the current 'as is' process being followed? If not, what are the discrepancies?
<--- Score

23. Has the direction changed at all during the course of competitive threats? If so, when did it change and

why?
<--- Score

24. Is data collected and displayed to better understand customer(s) critical needs and requirements.
<--- Score

25. Does the team have regular meetings?
<--- Score

26. Are audit criteria, scope, frequency and methods defined?
<--- Score

27. When is the estimated completion date?
<--- Score

28. Is the scope of competitive threats defined?
<--- Score

29. Scope of sensitive information?
<--- Score

30. How do you keep key subject matter experts in the loop?
<--- Score

31. Do the problem and goal statements meet the SMART criteria (specific, measurable, attainable, relevant, and time-bound)?
<--- Score

32. What baselines are required to be defined and managed?
<--- Score

33. How was the 'as is' process map developed, reviewed, verified and validated?
<--- Score

34. Is competitive threats currently on schedule according to the plan?
<--- Score

35. In what way can you redefine the criteria of choice clients have in your category in your favor?
<--- Score

36. What system do you use for gathering competitive threats information?
<--- Score

37. What is the scope?
<--- Score

38. How are consistent competitive threats definitions important?
<--- Score

39. What key stakeholder process output measure(s) does competitive threats leverage and how?
<--- Score

40. What is the definition of success?
<--- Score

41. What was the context?
<--- Score

42. What customer feedback methods were used to solicit their input?

<--- Score

43. Has/have the customer(s) been identified?
<--- Score

44. Has the improvement team collected the 'voice of the customer' (obtained feedback – qualitative and quantitative)?
<--- Score

45. Have all basic functions of competitive threats been defined?
<--- Score

46. The political context: who holds power?
<--- Score

47. Are there different segments of customers?
<--- Score

48. Has your scope been defined?
<--- Score

49. Will a competitive threats production readiness review be required?
<--- Score

50. Has everyone on the team, including the team leaders, been properly trained?
<--- Score

51. Is there a critical path to deliver competitive threats results?
<--- Score

52. Is competitive threats linked to key stakeholder

goals and objectives?
<--- Score

53. Has a project plan, Gantt chart, or similar been developed/completed?
<--- Score

54. How do you catch competitive threats definition inconsistencies?
<--- Score

55. Who are the competitive threats improvement team members, including Management Leads and Coaches?
<--- Score

56. What is in the scope and what is not in scope?
<--- Score

57. What is the worst case scenario?
<--- Score

58. Has the competitive threats work been fairly and/or equitably divided and delegated among team members who are qualified and capable to perform the work? Has everyone contributed?
<--- Score

59. Will team members regularly document their competitive threats work?
<--- Score

60. What are the competitive threats tasks and definitions?
<--- Score

61. Are the competitive threats requirements complete?
<--- Score

62. What competitive threats services do you require?
<--- Score

63. What are the competitive threats use cases?
<--- Score

64. How did the competitive threats manager receive input to the development of a competitive threats improvement plan and the estimated completion dates/times of each activity?
<--- Score

65. What would be the goal or target for a competitive threats's improvement team?
<--- Score

66. Are required metrics defined, what are they?
<--- Score

67. What are the record-keeping requirements of competitive threats activities?
<--- Score

68. How do you manage unclear competitive threats requirements?
<--- Score

69. What competitive threats requirements should be gathered?
<--- Score

70. What is a worst-case scenario for losses?

<--- Score

71. Has a team charter been developed and communicated?
<--- Score

72. Has a competitive threats requirement not been met?
<--- Score

73. What is in scope?
<--- Score

74. How and when will the baselines be defined?
<--- Score

75. What are the requirements for audit information?
<--- Score

76. Is the team equipped with available and reliable resources?
<--- Score

77. Are roles and responsibilities formally defined?
<--- Score

78. Will team members perform competitive threats work when assigned and in a timely fashion?
<--- Score

79. Where can you gather more information?
<--- Score

80. Has a high-level 'as is' process map been completed, verified and validated?
<--- Score

81. What are the Roles and Responsibilities for each team member and its leadership? Where is this documented?
<--- Score

82. How would you define competitive threats leadership?
<--- Score

83. If substitutes have been appointed, have they been briefed on the competitive threats goals and received regular communications as to the progress to date?
<--- Score

84. What is the context?
<--- Score

85. Is the team formed and are team leaders (Coaches and Management Leads) assigned?
<--- Score

86. Have all of the relationships been defined properly?
<--- Score

87. What are the compelling stakeholder reasons for embarking on competitive threats?
<--- Score

88. What are the rough order estimates on cost savings/opportunities that competitive threats brings?
<--- Score

89. What gets examined?

<--- Score

90. What are (control) requirements for competitive threats Information?

<--- Score

91. Is it clearly defined in and to your organization what you do?

<--- Score

92. Do you have a competitive threats success story or case study ready to tell and share?

<--- Score

93. How do you think the partners involved in competitive threats would have defined success?

<--- Score

94. Is there any additional competitive threats definition of success?

<--- Score

95. How do you gather competitive threats requirements?

<--- Score

96. Is there regularly 100% attendance at the team meetings? If not, have appointed substitutes attended to preserve cross-functionality and full representation?

<--- Score

97. Who is gathering information?

<--- Score

98. Who is gathering competitive threats information?
<--- Score

99. Is the team adequately staffed with the desired cross-functionality? If not, what additional resources are available to the team?
<--- Score

100. Is the improvement team aware of the different versions of a process: what they think it is vs. what it actually is vs. what it should be vs. what it could be?
<--- Score

101. What is the scope of the competitive threats effort?
<--- Score

102. Is full participation by members in regularly held team meetings guaranteed?
<--- Score

103. What sources do you use to gather information for a competitive threats study?
<--- Score

104. Are the competitive threats requirements testable?
<--- Score

105. What defines best in class?
<--- Score

106. How will the competitive threats team and the group measure complete success of competitive threats?
<--- Score

107. What critical content must be communicated –
who, what, when, where, and how?
<--- Score

108. Who defines (or who defined) the rules and roles?
<--- Score

**109. How do you manage changes in competitive
threats requirements?**
<--- Score

110. Are approval levels defined for contracts and
supplements to contracts?
<--- Score

111. What intelligence can you gather?
<--- Score

112. Is there a competitive threats management
charter, including stakeholder case, problem and
goal statements, scope, milestones, roles and
responsibilities, communication plan?
<--- Score

113. What is out of scope?
<--- Score

114. How do you manage scope?
<--- Score

115. Are customer(s) identified and segmented
according to their different needs and requirements?
<--- Score

116. Are there any constraints known that bear on the

ability to perform competitive threats work? How is the team addressing them?
<--- Score

117. What specifically is the problem? Where does it occur? When does it occur? What is its extent?
<--- Score

118. What are the dynamics of the communication plan?
<--- Score

119. Are improvement team members fully trained on competitive threats?
<--- Score

120. How would you define the culture at your organization, how susceptible is it to competitive threats changes?
<--- Score

121. Are different versions of process maps needed to account for the different types of inputs?
<--- Score

122. Is scope creep really all bad news?
<--- Score

123. Do you have organizational privacy requirements?
<--- Score

124. How is the team tracking and documenting its work?
<--- Score

125. Who approved the competitive threats scope?
<--- Score

126. Are all requirements met?
<--- Score

127. When is/was the competitive threats start date?
<--- Score

128. What is the scope of the competitive threats work?
<--- Score

129. Has anyone else (internal or external to the group) attempted to solve this problem or a similar one before? If so, what knowledge can be leveraged from these previous efforts?
<--- Score

130. Is the competitive threats scope complete and appropriately sized?
<--- Score

131. How do you hand over competitive threats context?
<--- Score

132. What are the core elements of the competitive threats business case?
<--- Score

133. Is there a clear competitive threats case definition?
<--- Score

134. What information do you gather?

<--- Score

135. What is the definition of competitive threats excellence?
<--- Score

136. What is out-of-scope initially?
<--- Score

137. What happens if competitive threats's scope changes?
<--- Score

138. How will variation in the actual durations of each activity be dealt with to ensure that the expected competitive threats results are met?
<--- Score

139. How do you gather the stories?
<--- Score

Add up total points for this section:
_ _ _ _ _ = Total points for this section

Divided by: _ _ _ _ _ _ (number of statements answered) = _ _ _ _ _ _
Average score for this section

Transfer your score to the competitive threats Index at the beginning of the Self-Assessment.

CRITERION #3: MEASURE:

INTENT: Gather the correct data.
Measure the current performance and
evolution of the situation.

In my belief, the answer to this
question is clearly defined:

5 Strongly Agree

4 Agree

3 Neutral

2 Disagree

1 Strongly Disagree

1. How do you verify and develop ideas and innovations?
<--- Score

2. Among the competitive threats product and service cost to be estimated, which is considered hardest to estimate?
<--- Score

3. How do you measure lifecycle phases?
<--- Score

4. Are there competing competitive threats priorities?
<--- Score

5. Is the solution cost-effective?
<--- Score

6. How sensitive must the competitive threats strategy be to cost?
<--- Score

7. What measurements are being captured?
<--- Score

8. Are the measurements objective?
<--- Score

9. How are measurements made?
<--- Score

10. What causes extra work or rework?
<--- Score

11. How frequently do you track competitive threats measures?
<--- Score

12. Are missed competitive threats opportunities costing your organization money?
<--- Score

13. What causes mismanagement?
<--- Score

14. What happens if cost savings do not materialize?
<--- Score

15. Are you able to realize any cost savings?
<--- Score

16. How to cause the change?
<--- Score

17. Are supply costs steady or fluctuating?
<--- Score

18. What measurements are possible, practicable and meaningful?
<--- Score

19. How will measures be used to manage and adapt?
<--- Score

20. What are the current costs of the competitive threats process?
<--- Score

21. What are the competitive threats key cost drivers?
<--- Score

22. What are the costs of reform?
<--- Score

23. What drives O&M cost?
<--- Score

24. How do you measure efficient delivery of competitive threats services?

<--- Score

25. What are the uncertainties surrounding estimates of impact?
<--- Score

26. Are the units of measure consistent?
<--- Score

27. What is measured? Why?
<--- Score

28. What does a Test Case verify?
<--- Score

29. What are your key competitive threats organizational performance measures, including key short and longer-term financial measures?
<--- Score

30. Does a competitive threats quantification method exist?
<--- Score

31. What is the total fixed cost?
<--- Score

32. Which competitive threats impacts are significant?
<--- Score

33. Was a business case (cost/benefit) developed?
<--- Score

34. How do you verify the authenticity of the data and information used?
<--- Score

35. Do you effectively measure and reward individual and team performance?
<--- Score

36. Where is the cost?
<--- Score

37. Have you included everything in your competitive threats cost models?
<--- Score

38. What are allowable costs?
<--- Score

39. How will you measure your competitive threats effectiveness?
<--- Score

40. What disadvantage does this cause for the user?
<--- Score

41. What are hidden competitive threats quality costs?
<--- Score

42. Who should receive measurement reports?
<--- Score

43. Which measures and indicators matter?
<--- Score

44. What tests verify requirements?
<--- Score

45. Are indirect costs charged to the competitive threats program?

<--- Score

46. What relevant entities could be measured?
<--- Score

47. How can you measure competitive threats in a systematic way?
<--- Score

48. What are the competitive threats investment costs?
<--- Score

49. What are the strategic priorities for this year?
<--- Score

50. What does losing customers cost your organization?
<--- Score

51. Have you made assumptions about the shape of the future, particularly its impact on your customers and competitors?
<--- Score

52. What would be a real cause for concern?
<--- Score

53. How do you control the overall costs of your work processes?
<--- Score

54. Are actual costs in line with budgeted costs?
<--- Score

55. What harm might be caused?

<--- Score

56. What is the cause of any competitive threats gaps?
<--- Score

57. How can you measure the performance?
<--- Score

58. How is performance measured?
<--- Score

59. How do you measure success?
<--- Score

60. How much does it cost?
<--- Score

61. How do you measure variability?
<--- Score

62. Is there an opportunity to verify requirements?
<--- Score

63. What are the types and number of measures to use?
<--- Score

64. When a disaster occurs, who gets priority?
<--- Score

65. How will effects be measured?
<--- Score

66. What is your decision requirements diagram?
<--- Score

67. What could cause you to change course?
<--- Score

68. How do you prevent mis-estimating cost?
<--- Score

69. How is the value delivered by competitive threats being measured?
<--- Score

70. What are the costs and benefits?
<--- Score

71. How will success or failure be measured?
<--- Score

72. How are costs allocated?
<--- Score

73. What does your operating model cost?
<--- Score

74. What are you verifying?
<--- Score

75. How will you measure success?
<--- Score

76. How is progress measured?
<--- Score

77. How do you quantify and qualify impacts?
<--- Score

78. What is the total cost related to deploying

competitive threats, including any consulting or professional services?
<--- Score

79. What is the cost of rework?
<--- Score

80. Why do you expend time and effort to implement measurement, for whom?
<--- Score

81. How do you verify and validate the competitive threats data?
<--- Score

82. Are there measurements based on task performance?
<--- Score

83. What are the operational costs after competitive threats deployment?
<--- Score

84. How do you verify your resources?
<--- Score

85. Do you aggressively reward and promote the people who have the biggest impact on creating excellent competitive threats services/products?
<--- Score

86. At what cost?
<--- Score

87. Do you have a flow diagram of what happens?
<--- Score

88. What are the costs of delaying competitive threats action?
<--- Score

89. What is the competitive threats business impact?
<--- Score

90. What causes investor action?
<--- Score

91. When should you bother with diagrams?
<--- Score

92. What are the costs?
<--- Score

93. What is the root cause(s) of the problem?
<--- Score

94. Is it possible to estimate the impact of unanticipated complexity such as wrong or failed assumptions, feedback, etcetera on proposed reforms?
<--- Score

95. What would it cost to replace your technology?
<--- Score

96. How can you reduce the costs of obtaining inputs?
<--- Score

97. Why do the measurements/indicators matter?
<--- Score

98. How do your measurements capture

actionable competitive threats information for use in exceeding your customers expectations and securing your customers engagement?

<--- Score

99. What are the estimated costs of proposed changes?

<--- Score

100. When are costs are incurred?

<--- Score

101. What potential environmental factors impact the competitive threats effort?

<--- Score

102. Are you aware of what could cause a problem?

<--- Score

103. What do people want to verify?

<--- Score

104. What users will be impacted?

<--- Score

105. What details are required of the competitive threats cost structure?

<--- Score

106. Does the competitive threats task fit the client's priorities?

<--- Score

107. How can a competitive threats test verify your ideas or assumptions?

<--- Score

108. How long to keep data and how to manage retention costs?
<--- Score

109. What are your operating costs?
<--- Score

110. Did you tackle the cause or the symptom?
<--- Score

111. What is an unallowable cost?
<--- Score

112. How can you reduce costs?
<--- Score

113. How do you verify performance?
<--- Score

114. What are your customers expectations and measures?
<--- Score

115. Where can you go to verify the info?
<--- Score

116. Do the benefits outweigh the costs?
<--- Score

117. What is your competitive threats quality cost segregation study?
<--- Score

118. How will your organization measure success?

<--- Score

119. Have design-to-cost goals been established?
<--- Score

120. Will competitive threats have an impact on current business continuity, disaster recovery processes and/or infrastructure?
<--- Score

121. Are competitive threats vulnerabilities categorized and prioritized?
<--- Score

122. What evidence is there and what is measured?
<--- Score

123. How will costs be allocated?
<--- Score

124. Are the competitive threats benefits worth its costs?
<--- Score

125. Do you have any cost competitive threats limitation requirements?
<--- Score

126. What causes innovation to fail or succeed in your organization?
<--- Score

127. Which costs should be taken into account?
<--- Score

128. How do you verify the competitive threats

requirements quality?
<--- Score

129. What can be used to verify compliance?
<--- Score

130. Who pays the cost?
<--- Score

131. How do you verify if competitive threats is built right?
<--- Score

132. What are your primary costs, revenues, assets?
<--- Score

133. Is the cost worth the competitive threats effort ?
<--- Score

134. What do you measure and why?
<--- Score

135. How can you manage cost down?
<--- Score

Add up total points for this section:
_ _ _ _ _ = Total points for this section

Divided by: _ _ _ _ _ _ (number of statements answered) = _ _ _ _ _ _
Average score for this section

Transfer your score to the competitive threats Index at the beginning of the Self-Assessment.

CRITERION #4: ANALYZE:

INTENT: Analyze causes, assumptions and hypotheses.

In my belief, the answer to this question is clearly defined:

5 Strongly Agree

4 Agree

3 Neutral

2 Disagree

1 Strongly Disagree

1. What will drive competitive threats change?
<--- Score

2. Who gets your output?
<--- Score

3. How do you promote understanding that opportunity for improvement is not criticism of the status quo, or the people who created the status quo?

<--- Score

4. Identify an operational issue in your organization, for example, could a particular task be done more quickly or more efficiently by competitive threats?
<--- Score

5. A compounding model resolution with available relevant data can often provide insight towards a solution methodology; which competitive threats models, tools and techniques are necessary?
<--- Score

6. What successful thing are you doing today that may be blinding you to new growth opportunities?
<--- Score

7. What qualifies as competition?
<--- Score

8. How are outputs preserved and protected?
<--- Score

9. Have any additional benefits been identified that will result from closing all or most of the gaps?
<--- Score

10. Do your employees have the opportunity to do what they do best everyday?
<--- Score

11. Do several people in different organizational units assist with the competitive threats process?
<--- Score

12. What qualifications do competitive threats leaders

need?
<--- Score

13. When should a process be art not science?
<--- Score

14. What are the revised rough estimates of the financial savings/opportunity for competitive threats improvements?
<--- Score

15. What, related to, competitive threats processes does your organization outsource?
<--- Score

16. How much data can be collected in the given timeframe?
<--- Score

17. What are the personnel training and qualifications required?
<--- Score

18. Do your contracts/agreements contain data security obligations?
<--- Score

19. Is data and process analysis, root cause analysis and quantifying the gap/opportunity in place?
<--- Score

20. What did the team gain from developing a sub-process map?
<--- Score

21. Where is competitive threats data gathered?

<--- Score

22. Who will facilitate the team and process?
<--- Score

23. Who qualifies to gain access to data?
<--- Score

24. What competitive threats data should be collected?
<--- Score

25. How often will data be collected for measures?
<--- Score

26. How can risk management be tied procedurally to process elements?
<--- Score

27. Were any designed experiments used to generate additional insight into the data analysis?
<--- Score

28. How is data used for program management and improvement?
<--- Score

29. Are you missing competitive threats opportunities?
<--- Score

30. What were the crucial 'moments of truth' on the process map?
<--- Score

31. Was a cause-and-effect diagram used to explore

the different types of causes (or sources of variation)?
<--- Score

32. What is your organizations system for selecting qualified vendors?
<--- Score

33. What is the competitive threats Driver?
<--- Score

34. What methods do you use to gather competitive threats data?
<--- Score

35. Are competitive threats changes recognized early enough to be approved through the regular process?
<--- Score

36. What resources go in to get the desired output?
<--- Score

37. What output to create?
<--- Score

38. Were Pareto charts (or similar) used to portray the 'heavy hitters' (or key sources of variation)?
<--- Score

39. How do you ensure that the competitive threats opportunity is realistic?
<--- Score

40. Who is involved with workflow mapping?
<--- Score

41. How will the change process be managed?

<--- Score

42. How is the way you as the leader think and process information affecting your organizational culture?
<--- Score

43. Can you add value to the current competitive threats decision-making process (largely qualitative) by incorporating uncertainty modeling (more quantitative)?
<--- Score

44. What kind of crime could a potential new hire have committed that would not only not disqualify him/her from being hired by your organization, but would actually indicate that he/she might be a particularly good fit?
<--- Score

45. Has data output been validated?
<--- Score

46. What are the competitive threats design outputs?
<--- Score

47. Were there any improvement opportunities identified from the process analysis?
<--- Score

48. What does the data say about the performance of the stakeholder process?
<--- Score

49. Record-keeping requirements flow from the records needed as inputs, outputs, controls and for transformation of a competitive threats process, are

the records needed as inputs to the competitive
threats process available?
<--- Score

50. What are your current levels and trends in key
competitive threats measures or indicators of product
and process performance that are important to and
directly serve your customers?
<--- Score

51. How is the data gathered?
<--- Score

52. What are the best opportunities for value
improvement?
<--- Score

53. Was a detailed process map created to amplify
critical steps of the 'as is' stakeholder process?
<--- Score

54. What competitive threats data will be collected?
<--- Score

55. Is the gap/opportunity displayed and
communicated in financial terms?
<--- Score

56. How do mission and objectives affect the
competitive threats processes of your organization?
<--- Score

57. What are the processes for audit reporting and
management?
<--- Score

58. What other organizational variables, such as reward systems or communication systems, affect the performance of this competitive threats process?
<--- Score

59. How do you identify specific competitive threats investment opportunities and emerging trends?
<--- Score

60. What data do you need to collect?
<--- Score

61. What qualifications and skills do you need?
<--- Score

62. What are your best practices for minimizing competitive threats project risk, while demonstrating incremental value and quick wins throughout the competitive threats project lifecycle?
<--- Score

63. How do your work systems and key work processes relate to and capitalize on your core competencies?
<--- Score

64. Are gaps between current performance and the goal performance identified?
<--- Score

65. How does the organization define, manage, and improve its competitive threats processes?
<--- Score

66. Has an output goal been set?

<--- Score

67. How difficult is it to qualify what competitive threats ROI is?
<--- Score

68. Where is the data coming from to measure compliance?
<--- Score

69. Do staff qualifications match your project?
<--- Score

70. What is the cost of poor quality as supported by the team's analysis?
<--- Score

71. Which competitive threats data should be retained?
<--- Score

72. Is the performance gap determined?
<--- Score

73. What tools were used to generate the list of possible causes?
<--- Score

74. Think about the functions involved in your competitive threats project, what processes flow from these functions?
<--- Score

75. What do you need to qualify?
<--- Score

76. How is competitive threats data gathered?
<--- Score

77. Do you, as a leader, bounce back quickly from setbacks?
<--- Score

78. What controls do you have in place to protect data?
<--- Score

79. Should you invest in industry-recognized qualifications?
<--- Score

80. Do you have the authority to produce the output?
<--- Score

81. What are your competitive threats processes?
<--- Score

82. What tools were used to narrow the list of possible causes?
<--- Score

83. How has the competitive threats data been gathered?
<--- Score

84. How do you implement and manage your work processes to ensure that they meet design requirements?
<--- Score

85. Are all staff in core competitive threats subjects Highly Qualified?

<--- Score

86. How was the detailed process map generated, verified, and validated?
<--- Score

87. What quality tools were used to get through the analyze phase?
<--- Score

88. Where can you get qualified talent today?
<--- Score

89. What is the Value Stream Mapping?
<--- Score

90. What qualifications are needed?
<--- Score

91. What training and qualifications will you need?
<--- Score

92. Is there any way to speed up the process?
<--- Score

93. Do you understand your management processes today?
<--- Score

94. How will the competitive threats data be captured?
<--- Score

95. What other jobs or tasks affect the performance of the steps in the competitive threats process?

<--- Score

96. Do your leaders quickly bounce back from setbacks?
<--- Score

97. How do you use competitive threats data and information to support organizational decision making and innovation?
<--- Score

98. Have the problem and goal statements been updated to reflect the additional knowledge gained from the analyze phase?
<--- Score

99. How is the competitive threats Value Stream Mapping managed?
<--- Score

100. Is the suppliers process defined and controlled?
<--- Score

101. What is your organizations process which leads to recognition of value generation?
<--- Score

102. What are your current levels and trends in key measures or indicators of competitive threats product and process performance that are important to and directly serve your customers? How do these results compare with the performance of your competitors and other organizations with similar offerings?
<--- Score

103. What are the disruptive competitive threats

technologies that enable your organization to radically change your business processes?
<--- Score

104. What conclusions were drawn from the team's data collection and analysis? How did the team reach these conclusions?
<--- Score

105. Do quality systems drive continuous improvement?
<--- Score

106. What are the necessary qualifications?
<--- Score

107. Did any value-added analysis or 'lean thinking' take place to identify some of the gaps shown on the 'as is' process map?
<--- Score

108. What process should you select for improvement?
<--- Score

109. Did any additional data need to be collected?
<--- Score

110. What are evaluation criteria for the output?
<--- Score

111. How will the data be checked for quality?
<--- Score

112. Have you defined which data is gathered how?
<--- Score

113. What types of data do your competitive threats indicators require?
<--- Score

114. Are your outputs consistent?
<--- Score

115. What are the competitive threats business drivers?
<--- Score

116. Who will gather what data?
<--- Score

117. What competitive threats metrics are outputs of the process?
<--- Score

118. Is there an established change management process?
<--- Score

119. What were the financial benefits resulting from any 'ground fruit or low-hanging fruit' (quick fixes)?
<--- Score

120. An organizationally feasible system request is one that considers the mission, goals and objectives of the organization, key questions are: is the competitive threats solution request practical and will it solve a problem or take advantage of an opportunity to achieve company goals?
<--- Score

121. What qualifications are necessary?
<--- Score

122. How do you measure the operational performance of your key work systems and processes, including productivity, cycle time, and other appropriate measures of process effectiveness, efficiency, and innovation?
<--- Score

123. Are all team members qualified for all tasks?
<--- Score

124. Who owns what data?
<--- Score

125. How many input/output points does it require?
<--- Score

126. What information qualified as important?
<--- Score

127. Is the required competitive threats data gathered?
<--- Score

128. What is the output?
<--- Score

129. What competitive threats data should be managed?
<--- Score

130. What are your outputs?
<--- Score

131. Is the final output clearly identified?
<--- Score

132. What systems/processes must you excel at?
<--- Score

133. What is the complexity of the output produced?
<--- Score

134. Is the competitive threats process severely
broken such that a re-design is necessary?
<--- Score

135. Is there a strict change management process?
<--- Score

Add up total points for this section:
_ _ _ _ _ = Total points for this section

Divided by: _ _ _ _ _ _ (number of
statements answered) = _ _ _ _ _ _
Average score for this section

Transfer your score to the competitive
threats Index at the beginning of the
Self-Assessment.

CRITERION #5: IMPROVE:

INTENT: Develop a practical solution. Innovate, establish and test the solution and to measure the results.

In my belief, the answer to this question is clearly defined:

5 Strongly Agree

4 Agree

3 Neutral

2 Disagree

1 Strongly Disagree

1. Why improve in the first place?
<--- Score

2. How does your organization evaluate strategic competitive threats success?
<--- Score

3. What competitive threats improvements can be made?

<--- Score

4. How do you improve your likelihood of success ?
<--- Score

5. What error proofing will be done to address some of the discrepancies observed in the 'as is' process?
<--- Score

6. Who will be using the results of the measurement activities?
<--- Score

7. What resources are required for the improvement efforts?
<--- Score

8. How do you decide how much to remunerate an employee?
<--- Score

9. How do you measure risk?
<--- Score

10. Who will be responsible for making the decisions to include or exclude requested changes once competitive threats is underway?
<--- Score

11. Who makes the competitive threats decisions in your organization?
<--- Score

12. How significant is the improvement in the eyes of the end user?
<--- Score

13. How risky is your organization?
<--- Score

14. What are the concrete competitive threats results?
<--- Score

15. Is there a high likelihood that any recommendations will achieve their intended results?
<--- Score

16. To what extent does management recognize competitive threats as a tool to increase the results?
<--- Score

17. How is continuous improvement applied to risk management?
<--- Score

18. What alternative responses are available to manage risk?
<--- Score

19. Which competitive threats solution is appropriate?
<--- Score

20. How do you manage competitive threats risk?
<--- Score

21. What criteria will you use to assess your competitive threats risks?
<--- Score

22. What area needs the greatest improvement?
<--- Score

23. At what point will vulnerability assessments be performed once competitive threats is put into production (e.g., ongoing Risk Management after implementation)?
<--- Score

24. Are risk triggers captured?
<--- Score

25. What were the criteria for evaluating a competitive threats pilot?
<--- Score

26. How do you define the solutions' scope?
<--- Score

27. Can the solution be designed and implemented within an acceptable time period?
<--- Score

28. What current systems have to be understood and/ or changed?
<--- Score

29. How do you measure progress and evaluate training effectiveness?
<--- Score

30. How do you improve productivity?
<--- Score

31. How scalable is your competitive threats solution?
<--- Score

32. Is the measure of success for competitive threats

understandable to a variety of people?
<--- Score

33. If you could go back in time five years, what decision would you make differently? What is your best guess as to what decision you're making today you might regret five years from now?
<--- Score

34. Is supporting competitive threats documentation required?
<--- Score

35. How will you know that a change is an improvement?
<--- Score

36. What can you do to improve?
<--- Score

37. What should a proof of concept or pilot accomplish?
<--- Score

38. Explorations of the frontiers of competitive threats will help you build influence, improve competitive threats, optimize decision making, and sustain change, what is your approach?
<--- Score

39. Who are the key stakeholders for the competitive threats evaluation?
<--- Score

40. How do you manage and improve your competitive threats work systems to deliver

customer value and achieve organizational success and sustainability?
<--- Score

41. In the past few months, what is the smallest change you have made that has had the biggest positive result? What was it about that small change that produced the large return?
<--- Score

42. What are the implications of the one critical competitive threats decision 10 minutes, 10 months, and 10 years from now?
<--- Score

43. What were the underlying assumptions on the cost-benefit analysis?
<--- Score

44. Was a competitive threats charter developed?
<--- Score

45. Is the competitive threats documentation thorough?
<--- Score

46. How can you better manage risk?
<--- Score

47. Who are the people involved in developing and implementing competitive threats?
<--- Score

48. Who manages competitive threats risk?
<--- Score

49. Would you develop a competitive threats Communication Strategy?
<--- Score

50. How will you know that you have improved?
<--- Score

51. What tools were used to tap into the creativity and encourage 'outside the box' thinking?
<--- Score

52. What do you want to improve?
<--- Score

53. Who will be responsible for documenting the competitive threats requirements in detail?
<--- Score

54. What are your current levels and trends in key measures or indicators of workforce and leader development?
<--- Score

55. Does the goal represent a desired result that can be measured?
<--- Score

56. Do vendor agreements bring new compliance risk ?
<--- Score

57. Will the controls trigger any other risks?
<--- Score

58. Are procedures documented for managing competitive threats risks?

<--- Score

59. How can you improve performance?
<--- Score

60. How can skill-level changes improve competitive threats?
<--- Score

61. What is competitive threats's impact on utilizing the best solution(s)?
<--- Score

62. What are the competitive threats security risks?
<--- Score

63. Is competitive threats documentation maintained?
<--- Score

64. What is the risk?
<--- Score

65. Which of the recognised risks out of all risks can be most likely transferred?
<--- Score

66. How does the team improve its work?
<--- Score

67. What tools do you use once you have decided on a competitive threats strategy and more importantly how do you choose?
<--- Score

68. What are the expected competitive threats results?
<--- Score

69. Can you integrate quality management and risk management?
<--- Score

70. What lessons, if any, from a pilot were incorporated into the design of the full-scale solution?
<--- Score

71. How will you measure the results?
<--- Score

72. What is competitive threats risk?
<--- Score

73. What tools were most useful during the improve phase?
<--- Score

74. Who should make the competitive threats decisions?
<--- Score

75. Does a good decision guarantee a good outcome?
<--- Score

76. What strategies for competitive threats improvement are successful?
<--- Score

77. When you map the key players in your own work and the types/domains of relationships with them, which relationships do you find easy and which challenging, and why?
<--- Score

78. How do you improve competitive threats service perception, and satisfaction?
<--- Score

79. How do you measure improved competitive threats service perception, and satisfaction?
<--- Score

80. What is the competitive threats's sustainability risk?
<--- Score

81. Is the competitive threats solution sustainable?
<--- Score

82. Do those selected for the competitive threats team have a good general understanding of what competitive threats is all about?
<--- Score

83. What actually has to improve and by how much?
<--- Score

84. Who controls the risk?
<--- Score

85. How will you recognize and celebrate results?
<--- Score

86. Is the competitive threats risk managed?
<--- Score

87. What practices helps your organization to develop its capacity to recognize patterns?
<--- Score

88. How do you deal with competitive threats risk?
<--- Score

89. Is the solution technically practical?
<--- Score

90. What risks do you need to manage?
<--- Score

91. What tools were used to evaluate the potential solutions?
<--- Score

92. How do you keep improving competitive threats?
<--- Score

93. What are the affordable competitive threats risks?
<--- Score

94. Who manages supplier risk management in your organization?
<--- Score

95. Are the most efficient solutions problem-specific?
<--- Score

96. Is risk periodically assessed?
<--- Score

97. competitive threats risk decisions: whose call Is It?
<--- Score

98. How are competitive threats risks managed?

<--- Score

99. Who controls key decisions that will be made?
<--- Score

100. Are you assessing competitive threats and risk?
<--- Score

101. How can the phases of competitive threats development be identified?
<--- Score

102. Do you need to do a usability evaluation?
<--- Score

103. For estimation problems, how do you develop an estimation statement?
<--- Score

104. Is the scope clearly documented?
<--- Score

105. How can you improve competitive threats?
<--- Score

106. What needs improvement? Why?
<--- Score

107. Is there any other competitive threats solution?
<--- Score

108. How do the competitive threats results compare with the performance of your competitors and other organizations with similar offerings?
<--- Score

109. Risk Identification: What are the possible risk events your organization faces in relation to competitive threats?
<--- Score

110. Who are the competitive threats decision-makers?
<--- Score

111. Where do you need competitive threats improvement?
<--- Score

112. Are events managed to resolution?
<--- Score

113. How do you link measurement and risk?
<--- Score

114. Have you identified breakpoints and/or risk tolerances that will trigger broad consideration of a potential need for intervention or modification of strategy?
<--- Score

115. Are decisions made in a timely manner?
<--- Score

116. How will you know when its improved?
<--- Score

117. Do you combine technical expertise with business knowledge and competitive threats Key topics include lifecycles, development approaches, requirements and how to make a business case?

<--- Score

118. Where do the competitive threats decisions reside?
<--- Score

119. What improvements have been achieved?
<--- Score

120. How do you mitigate competitive threats risk?
<--- Score

121. Risk factors: what are the characteristics of competitive threats that make it risky?
<--- Score

122. What is the implementation plan?
<--- Score

123. How are policy decisions made and where?
<--- Score

124. How do you go about comparing competitive threats approaches/solutions?
<--- Score

125. Risk events: what are the things that could go wrong?
<--- Score

126. Are risk management tasks balanced centrally and locally?
<--- Score

127. Have you achieved competitive threats improvements?

<--- Score

128. How is knowledge sharing about risk management improved?
<--- Score

129. Are the risks fully understood, reasonable and manageable?
<--- Score

130. What assumptions are made about the solution and approach?
<--- Score

131. Who do you report competitive threats results to?
<--- Score

132. What is the team's contingency plan for potential problems occurring in implementation?
<--- Score

Add up total points for this section:
_ _ _ _ _ = Total points for this section

Divided by: _ _ _ _ _ _ (number of statements answered) = _ _ _ _ _ _
Average score for this section

Transfer your score to the competitive threats Index at the beginning of the Self-Assessment.

CRITERION #6: CONTROL:

INTENT: Implement the practical solution. Maintain the performance and correct possible complications.

In my belief, the answer to this question is clearly defined:

5 Strongly Agree

4 Agree

3 Neutral

2 Disagree

1 Strongly Disagree

1. Is there a documented and implemented monitoring plan?
<--- Score

2. What should the next improvement project be that is related to competitive threats?
<--- Score

3. Is there documentation that will support the

successful operation of the improvement?
<--- Score

4. Will your goals reflect your program budget?
<--- Score

5. Is there a competitive threats Communication plan covering who needs to get what information when?
<--- Score

6. Are the competitive threats standards challenging?
<--- Score

7. Does the response plan contain a definite closed loop continual improvement scheme (e.g., plan-do-check-act)?
<--- Score

8. Do the viable solutions scale to future needs?
<--- Score

9. Implementation Planning: is a pilot needed to test the changes before a full roll out occurs?
<--- Score

10. Do the competitive threats decisions you make today help people and the planet tomorrow?
<--- Score

11. What do you stand for--and what are you against?
<--- Score

12. How will input, process, and output variables be checked to detect for sub-optimal conditions?
<--- Score

13. How do controls support value?

<--- Score

14. What is your theory of human motivation, and how does your compensation plan fit with that view?

<--- Score

15. What competitive threats standards are applicable?

<--- Score

16. How do senior leaders actions reflect a commitment to the organizations competitive threats values?

<--- Score

17. Has the improved process and its steps been standardized?

<--- Score

18. What adjustments to the strategies are needed?

<--- Score

19. What quality tools were useful in the control phase?

<--- Score

20. Is a response plan established and deployed?

<--- Score

21. Are there documented procedures?

<--- Score

22. How can you best use all of your knowledge repositories to enhance learning and sharing?

<--- Score

23. Who has control over resources?
<--- Score

24. What is the standard for acceptable competitive threats performance?
<--- Score

25. How widespread is its use?
<--- Score

26. What are the performance and scale of the competitive threats tools?
<--- Score

27. How do you establish and deploy modified action plans if circumstances require a shift in plans and rapid execution of new plans?
<--- Score

28. Are documented procedures clear and easy to follow for the operators?
<--- Score

29. Are you measuring, monitoring and predicting competitive threats activities to optimize operations and profitability, and enhancing outcomes?
<--- Score

30. Who sets the competitive threats standards?
<--- Score

31. How do you monitor usage and cost?
<--- Score

32. Can you adapt and adjust to changing competitive threats situations?
<--- Score

33. Against what alternative is success being measured?
<--- Score

34. Act/Adjust: What Do you Need to Do Differently?
<--- Score

35. Who is the competitive threats process owner?
<--- Score

36. What should you measure to verify efficiency gains?
<--- Score

37. What are the critical parameters to watch?
<--- Score

38. Is there a recommended audit plan for routine surveillance inspections of competitive threats's gains?
<--- Score

39. Does competitive threats appropriately measure and monitor risk?
<--- Score

40. Is new knowledge gained imbedded in the response plan?
<--- Score

41. Will existing staff require re-training, for

example, to learn new business processes?
<--- Score

42. Who is going to spread your message?
<--- Score

43. Where do ideas that reach policy makers and planners as proposals for competitive threats strengthening and reform actually originate?
<--- Score

44. Is there a transfer of ownership and knowledge to process owner and process team tasked with the responsibilities.
<--- Score

45. How will the process owner verify improvement in present and future sigma levels, process capabilities?
<--- Score

46. What other systems, operations, processes, and infrastructures (hiring practices, staffing, training, incentives/rewards, metrics/dashboards/scorecards, etc.) need updates, additions, changes, or deletions in order to facilitate knowledge transfer and improvements?
<--- Score

47. What is your plan to assess your security risks?
<--- Score

48. You may have created your quality measures at a time when you lacked resources, technology wasn't up to the required standard, or low service levels were the industry norm. Have those circumstances changed?

<--- Score

49. Have new or revised work instructions resulted?
<--- Score

50. How do you plan on providing proper recognition and disclosure of supporting companies?
<--- Score

51. Do you monitor the effectiveness of your competitive threats activities?
<--- Score

52. How will report readings be checked to effectively monitor performance?
<--- Score

53. Is knowledge gained on process shared and institutionalized?
<--- Score

54. Are the planned controls working?
<--- Score

55. What can you control?
<--- Score

56. What are you attempting to measure/monitor?
<--- Score

57. Is a response plan in place for when the input, process, or output measures indicate an 'out-of-control' condition?
<--- Score

58. Are operating procedures consistent?
<--- Score

59. How might the group capture best practices and lessons learned so as to leverage improvements?
<--- Score

60. Are controls in place and consistently applied?
<--- Score

61. What are your results for key measures or indicators of the accomplishment of your competitive threats strategy and action plans, including building and strengthening core competencies?
<--- Score

62. How do you encourage people to take control and responsibility?
<--- Score

63. Is there a control plan in place for sustaining improvements (short and long-term)?
<--- Score

64. How will new or emerging customer needs/requirements be checked/communicated to orient the process toward meeting the new specifications and continually reducing variation?
<--- Score

65. Will any special training be provided for results interpretation?
<--- Score

66. Is the competitive threats test/monitoring cost

justified?
<--- Score

67. Are suggested corrective/restorative actions indicated on the response plan for known causes to problems that might surface?
<--- Score

68. Does the competitive threats performance meet the customer's requirements?
<--- Score

69. What is the best design framework for competitive threats organization now that, in a post industrial-age if the top-down, command and control model is no longer relevant?
<--- Score

70. What other areas of the group might benefit from the competitive threats team's improvements, knowledge, and learning?
<--- Score

71. What are the key elements of your competitive threats performance improvement system, including your evaluation, organizational learning, and innovation processes?
<--- Score

72. Can support from partners be adjusted?
<--- Score

73. How will the process owner and team be able to hold the gains?
<--- Score

74. How will you measure your QA plan's effectiveness?
<--- Score

75. Is there a standardized process?
<--- Score

76. How do you plan for the cost of succession?
<--- Score

77. What key inputs and outputs are being measured on an ongoing basis?
<--- Score

78. How do your controls stack up?
<--- Score

79. What are customers monitoring?
<--- Score

80. Does a troubleshooting guide exist or is it needed?
<--- Score

81. What is the recommended frequency of auditing?
<--- Score

82. Is reporting being used or needed?
<--- Score

83. What is the control/monitoring plan?
<--- Score

84. Is there an action plan in case of emergencies?
<--- Score

85. Are pertinent alerts monitored, analyzed and

distributed to appropriate personnel?
<--- Score

86. Who will be in control?
<--- Score

87. What do your reports reflect?
<--- Score

88. Do you monitor the competitive threats decisions made and fine tune them as they evolve?
<--- Score

89. How do you select, collect, align, and integrate competitive threats data and information for tracking daily operations and overall organizational performance, including progress relative to strategic objectives and action plans?
<--- Score

90. How will competitive threats decisions be made and monitored?
<--- Score

91. Are new process steps, standards, and documentation ingrained into normal operations?
<--- Score

92. Does job training on the documented procedures need to be part of the process team's education and training?
<--- Score

93. Who controls critical resources?
<--- Score

94. Has the competitive threats value of standards been quantified?
<--- Score

95. In the case of a competitive threats project, the criteria for the audit derive from implementation objectives, an audit of a competitive threats project involves assessing whether the recommendations outlined for implementation have been met, can you track that any competitive threats project is implemented as planned, and is it working?
<--- Score

96. How will the day-to-day responsibilities for monitoring and continual improvement be transferred from the improvement team to the process owner?
<--- Score

97. Are the planned controls in place?
<--- Score

Add up total points for this section:
_ _ _ _ _ = Total points for this section

Divided by: _ _ _ _ _ _ (number of statements answered) = _ _ _ _ _ _
Average score for this section

Transfer your score to the competitive threats Index at the beginning of the Self-Assessment.

CRITERION #7: SUSTAIN:

INTENT: Retain the benefits.

In my belief, the answer to this
question is clearly defined:

5 Strongly Agree

4 Agree

3 Neutral

2 Disagree

1 Strongly Disagree

1. What business benefits will competitive threats
goals deliver if achieved?
<--- Score

2. What are the essentials of internal competitive
threats management?
<--- Score

3. Are assumptions made in competitive threats
stated explicitly?
<--- Score

4. What is the funding source for this project?
<--- Score

5. What is a feasible sequencing of reform initiatives over time?
<--- Score

6. How do you provide a safe environment -physically and emotionally?
<--- Score

7. What are specific competitive threats rules to follow?
<--- Score

8. Are you relevant? Will you be relevant five years from now? Ten?
<--- Score

9. What are the barriers to increased competitive threats production?
<--- Score

10. Has implementation been effective in reaching specified objectives so far?
<--- Score

11. Are new benefits received and understood?
<--- Score

12. Is there any reason to believe the opposite of my current belief?
<--- Score

13. What is an unauthorized commitment?

<--- Score

14. Are you making progress, and are you making progress as competitive threats leaders?
<--- Score

15. Do you have the right capabilities and capacities?
<--- Score

16. How do you engage the workforce, in addition to satisfying them?
<--- Score

17. Which models, tools and techniques are necessary?
<--- Score

18. Political -is anyone trying to undermine this project?
<--- Score

19. What is the kind of project structure that would be appropriate for your competitive threats project, should it be formal and complex, or can it be less formal and relatively simple?
<--- Score

20. Do you say no to customers for no reason?
<--- Score

21. How do senior leaders deploy your organizations vision and values through your leadership system, to the workforce, to key suppliers and partners, and to customers and other stakeholders, as appropriate?
<--- Score

22. What unique value proposition (UVP) do you offer?
<--- Score

23. Is your basic point _____ or _____?
<--- Score

24. How do you transition from the baseline to the target?
<--- Score

25. Whom among your colleagues do you trust, and for what?
<--- Score

26. Which competitive threats goals are the most important?
<--- Score

27. How do you assess the competitive threats pitfalls that are inherent in implementing it?
<--- Score

28. What information is critical to your organization that your executives are ignoring?
<--- Score

29. Who is on the team?
<--- Score

30. What did you miss in the interview for the worst hire you ever made?
<--- Score

31. How do you cross-sell and up-sell your competitive threats success?

<--- Score

32. Do competitive threats rules make a reasonable demand on a users capabilities?
<--- Score

33. Do you think competitive threats accomplishes the goals you expect it to accomplish?
<--- Score

34. Why should you adopt a competitive threats framework?
<--- Score

35. How is implementation research currently incorporated into each of your goals?
<--- Score

36. What would have to be true for the option on the table to be the best possible choice?
<--- Score

37. Do you know who is a friend or a foe?
<--- Score

38. How do you set competitive threats stretch targets and how do you get people to not only participate in setting these stretch targets but also that they strive to achieve these?
<--- Score

39. How do you proactively clarify deliverables and competitive threats quality expectations?
<--- Score

40. Who do you want your customers to become?

<--- Score

41. Who uses your product in ways you never expected?
<--- Score

42. Is maximizing competitive threats protection the same as minimizing competitive threats loss?
<--- Score

43. Who do we want your customers to become?
<--- Score

44. Which individuals, teams or departments will be involved in competitive threats?
<--- Score

45. If you got fired and a new hire took your place, what would she do different?
<--- Score

46. Do you have the right people on the bus?
<--- Score

47. What have been your experiences in defining long range competitive threats goals?
<--- Score

48. How likely is it that a customer would recommend your company to a friend or colleague?
<--- Score

49. What are the usability implications of competitive threats actions?
<--- Score

50. What you are going to do to affect the numbers?
<--- Score

51. What projects are going on in the organization today, and what resources are those projects using from the resource pools?
<--- Score

52. What counts that you are not counting?
<--- Score

53. Are you using a design thinking approach and integrating Innovation, competitive threats Experience, and Brand Value?
<--- Score

54. What could happen if you do not do it?
<--- Score

55. In a project to restructure competitive threats outcomes, which stakeholders would you involve?
<--- Score

56. Do you know what you are doing? And who do you call if you don't?
<--- Score

57. Who are your customers?
<--- Score

58. Can the schedule be done in the given time?
<--- Score

59. How can you incorporate support to ensure safe and effective use of competitive threats into the services that you provide?

<--- Score

60. How do you accomplish your long range competitive threats goals?
<--- Score

61. Why do and why don't your customers like your organization?
<--- Score

62. Think of your competitive threats project, what are the main functions?
<--- Score

63. Who is responsible for ensuring appropriate resources (time, people and money) are allocated to competitive threats?
<--- Score

64. When information truly is ubiquitous, when reach and connectivity are completely global, when computing resources are infinite, and when a whole new set of impossibilities are not only possible, but happening, what will that do to your business?
<--- Score

65. What would you recommend your friend do if he/she were facing this dilemma?
<--- Score

66. What is the source of the strategies for competitive threats strengthening and reform?
<--- Score

67. What may be the consequences for the performance of an organization if all stakeholders are

not consulted regarding competitive threats?
<--- Score

68. Instead of going to current contacts for new ideas, what if you reconnected with dormant contacts-- the people you used to know? If you were going reactivate a dormant tie, who would it be?
<--- Score

69. How can you become the company that would put you out of business?
<--- Score

70. Are you / should you be revolutionary or evolutionary?
<--- Score

71. Who do you think the world wants your organization to be?
<--- Score

72. Who will manage the integration of tools?
<--- Score

73. Who, on the executive team or the board, has spoken to a customer recently?
<--- Score

74. What have you done to protect your business from competitive encroachment?
<--- Score

75. How will you know that the competitive threats project has been successful?
<--- Score

76. What are the challenges?
<--- Score

77. How do you maintain competitive threats's
Integrity?
<--- Score

78. How do you foster innovation?
<--- Score

79. What one word do you want to own in the minds
of your customers, employees, and partners?
<--- Score

80. Why should people listen to you?
<--- Score

81. How do you know if you are successful?
<--- Score

82. To whom do you add value?
<--- Score

83. What relationships among competitive threats
trends do you perceive?
<--- Score

**84. Are you satisfied with your current role? If not,
what is missing from it?**
<--- Score

85. Where can you break convention?
<--- Score

86. Can you maintain your growth without detracting
from the factors that have contributed to your

success?

<--- Score

87. If you had to leave your organization for a year and the only communication you could have with employees/colleagues was a single paragraph, what would you write?

<--- Score

88. Who is the main stakeholder, with ultimate responsibility for driving competitive threats forward?

<--- Score

89. How much does competitive threats help?

<--- Score

90. Are the assumptions believable and achievable?

<--- Score

91. Will it be accepted by users?

<--- Score

92. Did your employees make progress today?

<--- Score

93. How do you go about securing competitive threats?

<--- Score

94. Is the competitive threats organization completing tasks effectively and efficiently?

<--- Score

95. Do you have past competitive threats successes?

<--- Score

96. If you had to rebuild your organization without any traditional competitive advantages (i.e., no killer technology, promising research, innovative product/ service delivery model, etcetera), how would your people have to approach their work and collaborate together in order to create the necessary conditions for success?
<--- Score

97. What does your signature ensure?
<--- Score

98. Is there a work around that you can use?
<--- Score

99. Are the criteria for selecting recommendations stated?
<--- Score

100. How can you negotiate competitive threats successfully with a stubborn boss, an irate client, or a deceitful coworker?
<--- Score

101. Which functions and people interact with the supplier and or customer?
<--- Score

102. What trophy do you want on your mantle?
<--- Score

103. How much contingency will be available in the budget?
<--- Score

104. What is your formula for success in competitive threats ?
<--- Score

105. Will there be any necessary staff changes (redundancies or new hires)?
<--- Score

106. Are your responses positive or negative?
<--- Score

107. Have benefits been optimized with all key stakeholders?
<--- Score

108. What competitive threats modifications can you make work for you?
<--- Score

109. What is effective competitive threats?
<--- Score

110. What knowledge, skills and characteristics mark a good competitive threats project manager?
<--- Score

111. What goals did you miss?
<--- Score

112. What is the craziest thing you can do?
<--- Score

113. In retrospect, of the projects that you pulled the plug on, what percent do you wish had been allowed to keep going, and what percent do you wish had ended earlier?

<--- Score

114. At what moment would you think; Will I get fired?
<--- Score

115. What happens if you do not have enough funding?
<--- Score

116. What are current competitive threats paradigms?
<--- Score

117. Are all key stakeholders present at all Structured Walkthroughs?
<--- Score

118. Are you changing as fast as the world around you?
<--- Score

119. What new services of functionality will be implemented next with competitive threats ?
<--- Score

120. Who else should you help?
<--- Score

121. How will you ensure you get what you expected?
<--- Score

122. Is it economical; do you have the time and money?
<--- Score

123. How do you keep records, of what?
<--- Score

124. What is it like to work for you?
<--- Score

125. Have new benefits been realized?
<--- Score

126. How do you ensure that implementations of competitive threats products are done in a way that ensures safety?
<--- Score

127. Would you rather sell to knowledgeable and informed customers or to uninformed customers?
<--- Score

128. Why is it important to have senior management support for a competitive threats project?
<--- Score

129. What will be the consequences to the stakeholder (financial, reputation etc) if competitive threats does not go ahead or fails to deliver the objectives?
<--- Score

130. Whose voice (department, ethnic group, women, older workers, etc) might you have missed hearing from in your company, and how might you amplify this voice to create positive momentum for your business?
<--- Score

131. What are the short and long-term competitive threats goals?
<--- Score

132. What are you challenging?
<--- Score

133. What is the range of capabilities?
<--- Score

134. What is your competitive threats strategy?
<--- Score

135. How do you lead with competitive threats in mind?
<--- Score

136. Is a competitive threats team work effort in place?
<--- Score

137. Are you maintaining a past–present–future perspective throughout the competitive threats discussion?
<--- Score

138. Can you do all this work?
<--- Score

139. What role does communication play in the success or failure of a competitive threats project?
<--- Score

140. How do you govern and fulfill your societal responsibilities?
<--- Score

141. Do you have enough freaky customers in your portfolio pushing you to the limit day in and day out?
<--- Score

142. How do you track customer value, profitability or financial return, organizational success, and sustainability?
<--- Score

143. What are the gaps in your knowledge and experience?
<--- Score

144. How do you foster the skills, knowledge, talents, attributes, and characteristics you want to have?
<--- Score

145. Why not do competitive threats?
<--- Score

146. What are strategies for increasing support and reducing opposition?
<--- Score

147. What are the success criteria that will indicate that competitive threats objectives have been met and the benefits delivered?
<--- Score

148. What are internal and external competitive threats relations?
<--- Score

149. What potential megatrends could make your

business model obsolete?
<--- Score

150. What is the overall talent health of your organization as a whole at senior levels, and for each organization reporting to a member of the Senior Leadership Team?
<--- Score

151. Who have you, as a company, historically been when you've been at your best?
<--- Score

152. Can you break it down?
<--- Score

153. What is the overall business strategy?
<--- Score

154. Do you see more potential in people than they do in themselves?
<--- Score

155. Ask yourself: how would you do this work if you only had one staff member to do it?
<--- Score

156. What are the rules and assumptions your industry operates under? What if the opposite were true?
<--- Score

157. What was the last experiment you ran?
<--- Score

158. What threat is competitive threats addressing?

<--- Score

159. How do you listen to customers to obtain actionable information?
<--- Score

160. If you find that you havent accomplished one of the goals for one of the steps of the competitive threats strategy, what will you do to fix it?
<--- Score

161. Who will be responsible for deciding whether competitive threats goes ahead or not after the initial investigations?
<--- Score

162. What are your most important goals for the strategic competitive threats objectives?
<--- Score

163. What are your personal philosophies regarding competitive threats and how do they influence your work?
<--- Score

164. Who will determine interim and final deadlines?
<--- Score

165. Is competitive threats realistic, or are you setting yourself up for failure?
<--- Score

166. What are the potential basics of competitive threats fraud?
<--- Score

167. Are there any activities that you can take off your to do list?
<--- Score

168. What is your BATNA (best alternative to a negotiated agreement)?
<--- Score

169. Is a competitive threats breakthrough on the horizon?
<--- Score

170. How are you doing compared to your industry?
<--- Score

171. Is your strategy driving your strategy? Or is the way in which you allocate resources driving your strategy?
<--- Score

172. Do you feel that more should be done in the competitive threats area?
<--- Score

173. What do we do when new problems arise?
<--- Score

174. In the past year, what have you done (or could you have done) to increase the accurate perception of your company/brand as ethical and honest?
<--- Score

175. What is your competitive advantage?
<--- Score

176. What is the estimated value of the project?
<--- Score

177. What are the business goals competitive threats is aiming to achieve?
<--- Score

178. Who are the key stakeholders?
<--- Score

179. How important is competitive threats to the user organizations mission?
<--- Score

180. If you do not follow, then how to lead?
<--- Score

181. If no one would ever find out about your accomplishments, how would you lead differently?
<--- Score

182. Marketing budgets are tighter, consumers are more skeptical, and social media has changed forever the way we talk about competitive threats, how do you gain traction?
<--- Score

183. How does competitive threats integrate with other stakeholder initiatives?
<--- Score

184. What stupid rule would you most like to kill?
<--- Score

185. Who is responsible for errors?

<--- Score

186. How long will it take to change?
<--- Score

187. Do you have an implicit bias for capital investments over people investments?
<--- Score

188. How will you motivate the stakeholders with the least vested interest?
<--- Score

189. Is the impact that competitive threats has shown?
<--- Score

190. Operational - will it work?
<--- Score

191. How do you determine the key elements that affect competitive threats workforce satisfaction, how are these elements determined for different workforce groups and segments?
<--- Score

192. Were lessons learned captured and communicated?
<--- Score

193. Do you think you know, or do you know you know ?
<--- Score

194. How do you make it meaningful in connecting competitive threats with what users do day-to-

day?

<--- Score

195. Is competitive threats dependent on the successful delivery of a current project?

<--- Score

196. How do you deal with competitive threats changes?

<--- Score

197. Who are four people whose careers you have enhanced?

<--- Score

198. How do you create buy-in?

<--- Score

199. What is something you believe that nearly no one agrees with you on?

<--- Score

200. If you were responsible for initiating and implementing major changes in your organization, what steps might you take to ensure acceptance of those changes?

<--- Score

201. How do customers see your organization?

<--- Score

202. Is there any existing competitive threats governance structure?

<--- Score

203. What happens at your organization when people

fail?

<--- Score

204. What is your question? Why?

<--- Score

205. What trouble can you get into?

<--- Score

206. What are you trying to prove to yourself, and how might it be hijacking your life and business success?

<--- Score

207. Are you paying enough attention to the partners your company depends on to succeed?

<--- Score

208. What is the recommended frequency of auditing?

<--- Score

209. How do you stay inspired?

<--- Score

210. What is the purpose of competitive threats in relation to the mission?

<--- Score

211. What are the long-term competitive threats goals?

<--- Score

212. What management system can you use to leverage the competitive threats experience, ideas, and concerns of the people closest to the work to be

done?
<--- Score

213. What are the top 3 things at the forefront of your competitive threats agendas for the next 3 years?
<--- Score

Add up total points for this section:
_____ = Total points for this section

Divided by: _____ (number of statements answered) = _____
Average score for this section

Transfer your score to the competitive threats Index at the beginning of the Self-Assessment.

Competitive Threats and Managing Projects, Criteria for Project Managers:

1.0 Initiating Process Group: Competitive Threats

1. What are the tools and techniques to be used in each phase?

2. What business situation is being addressed?

3. Do you understand the quality and control criteria that must be achieved for successful Competitive Threats project completion?

4. Will the Competitive Threats project meet the client requirements, and will it achieve the business success criteria that justified doing the Competitive Threats project in the first place?

5. How is each deliverable reviewed, verified, and validated?

6. What will be the pressing issues of tomorrow?

7. What will you do to minimize the impact should a risk event occur?

8. What are the overarching issues of your organization?

9. Do you know all the stakeholders impacted by the Competitive Threats project and what needs are?

10. Did the Competitive Threats project team have the right skills?

11. What are the short and long term implications?

12. At which cmmi level are software processes documented, standardized, and integrated into a standard to-be practiced process for your organization?

13. If the risk event occurs, what will you do?

14. Which of six sigmas dmaic phases focuses on the measurement of internal process that affect factors that are critical to quality?

15. Are the Competitive Threats project team and stakeholders meeting regularly and using a meeting agenda and taking notes to accurately document what is being covered and what happened in the weekly meetings?

16. Were resources available as planned?

17. Who supports, improves, and oversees standardized processes related to the Competitive Threats projects program?

18. First of all, should any action be taken?

19. If action is called for, what form should it take?

20. What are the required resources?

1.1 Project Charter: Competitive Threats

21. Are you building in-house ?

22. Why Outsource?

23. Customer: who are you doing the Competitive Threats project for?

24. For whom?

25. When is a charter needed?

26. Why do you manage integration?

27. Did your Competitive Threats project ask for this?

28. Are there special technology requirements?

29. Run it as as a startup?

30. When?

31. When do you use a Competitive Threats project Charter?

32. Where and how does the team fit within your organization structure?

33. Who is the Competitive Threats project Manager?

34. Why is it important?

35. Customer benefits: what customer requirements does this Competitive Threats project address?

36. Who manages integration?

37. Why the improvements?

38. Success determination factors: how will the success of the Competitive Threats project be determined from the customers perspective?

39. What outcome, in measureable terms, are you hoping to accomplish?

40. Fit with other Products Compliments – Cannibalizes?

1.2 Stakeholder Register: Competitive Threats

41. How much influence do they have on the Competitive Threats project?

42. Who is managing stakeholder engagement?

43. What opportunities exist to provide communications?

44. Who wants to talk about Security?

45. What is the power of the stakeholder?

46. What are the major Competitive Threats project milestones requiring communications or providing communications opportunities?

47. How should employers make voices heard?

48. What & Why?

49. Who are the stakeholders?

50. How will reports be created?

51. How big is the gap?

52. Is your organization ready for change?

1.3 Stakeholder Analysis Matrix: Competitive Threats

53. Who is most dependent on the resources at stake?

54. Sustainable financial backing?

55. How are the threatened Competitive Threats project targets being used?

56. Arena: in what fields are the actors active, where are they present?

57. Who has been involved in the area (thematic or geographic) in the past?

58. Organizational Applicability?

59. What organizational arrangements are planned to ensure the Competitive Threats project achieves its social development outcomes?

60. How to measure the achievement of the Development Objective?

61. Which conditions out of the control of the management are crucial for the achievement of the immediate objective?

62. Processes and systems, etc?

63. How affected by the problem(s)?

64. Competitive advantages?

65. What obstacles does your organization face?

66. Are the interests in line with the program objectives?

67. Which resources are required?

68. How to involve media?

69. Loss of key staff?

70. How much do resources cost?

71. What should thwe organizations stakeholders avoid?

72. Management cover, succession?

2.0 Planning Process Group: Competitive Threats

73. What makes your Competitive Threats project successful?

74. How should needs be met?

75. In what way has the Competitive Threats project come up with innovative measures for problem-solving?

76. When will the Competitive Threats project be done?

77. How well did the chosen processes fit the needs of the Competitive Threats project?

78. How does activity resource estimation affect activity duration estimation?

79. What is the critical path for this Competitive Threats project, and what is the duration of the critical path?

80. Professionals want to know what is expected from them; what are the deliverables?

81. How are it Competitive Threats projects different?

82. Product breakdown structure (pbs): what is the Competitive Threats project result or product, and how should it look like, what are its parts?

83. How will it affect you?

84. What will you do?

85. To what extent and in what ways are the Competitive Threats project contributing to progress towards organizational reform?

86. When developing the estimates for Competitive Threats project phases, you choose to add the individual estimates for the activities that comprise each phase. What type of estimation method are you using?

87. Is the schedule for the set products being met?

88. How do you integrate Competitive Threats project Planning with the Iterative/Evolutionary SDLC?

89. What do you need to do?

90. If task x starts two days late, what is the effect on the Competitive Threats project end date?

2.1 Project Management Plan: Competitive Threats

91. What are the known stakeholder requirements?

92. Is the appropriate plan selected based on your organizations objectives and evaluation criteria expressed in Principles and Guidelines policies?

93. Is the engineering content at a feasibility level-of-detail, and is it sufficiently complete, to provide an adequate basis for the baseline cost estimate?

94. Development trends and opportunities. What if the positive direction and vision of your organization causes expected trends to change?

95. What did not work so well?

96. What should you drop in order to add something new?

97. When is a Competitive Threats project management plan created?

98. Are the existing and future without-plan conditions reasonable and appropriate?

99. Is the budget realistic?

100. Does the implementation plan have an appropriate division of responsibilities?

101. How do you manage time?

102. Is mitigation authorized or recommended?

103. What are the training needs?

104. Are alternatives safe, functional, constructible, economical, reasonable and sustainable?

105. What is the business need?

106. What are the assigned resources?

107. Are cost risk analysis methods applied to develop contingencies for the estimated total Competitive Threats project costs?

108. Will you add a schedule and diagram?

109. What happened during the process that you found interesting?

110. What are the constraints?

2.2 Scope Management Plan: Competitive Threats

111. Has a proper Competitive Threats project work location been established that will allow the team to work together with user personnel?

112. What is the unique product, service or result?

113. Are you meeting with stake holders and team members?

114. Where do scope management processes fit in?

115. Have adequate resources been provided by management to ensure Competitive Threats project success?

116. Has process improvement efforts been completed before requirements efforts begin?

117. Are the budget estimates reasonable?

118. Is there a formal set of procedures supporting Issues Management?

119. Is there a formal process for updating the Competitive Threats project baseline?

120. Has a capability assessment been conducted?

121. Has the Competitive Threats project scope been baselined?

122. Is there a Steering Committee in place?

123. Is current scope of the Competitive Threats project substantially different than that originally defined?

124. Would the Competitive Threats project cost sharing involve reimbursement to the sponsor?

125. Will the Competitive Threats project deliverables become accepted in writing?

126. Are staffing resource estimates sufficiently detailed and documented for use in planning and tracking the Competitive Threats project?

127. Has the selected plan been formulated using cost effectiveness and incremental analysis techniques?

128. Are funding resource estimates sufficiently detailed and documented for use in planning and tracking the Competitive Threats project?

2.3 Requirements Management Plan: Competitive Threats

129. Will you use tracing to help understand the impact of a change in requirements?

130. Is there formal agreement on who has authority to request a change in requirements?

131. Who came up with this requirement?

132. What is a problem?

133. Will you have access to stakeholders when you need them?

134. Who will do the reporting and to whom will reports be delivered?

135. Did you get proper approvals?

136. Will you perform a Requirements Risk assessment and develop a plan to deal with risks?

137. Did you use declarative statements?

138. Is the system software (non-operating system) new to the IT Competitive Threats project team?

139. What information regarding the Competitive Threats project requirements will be reported?

140. Who will finally present the work or product(s) for

acceptance?

141. How will you develop the schedule of requirements activities?

142. How knowledgeable is the team in the proposed application area?

143. What went right?

144. Who will approve the requirements (and if multiple approvers, in what order)?

145. Is there formal agreement on who has authority to approve a change in requirements?

146. Will you document changes to requirements?

147. Did you provide clear and concise specifications?

148. Who will perform the analysis?

2.4 Requirements Documentation: Competitive Threats

149. Does your organization restrict technical alternatives?

150. What are the potential disadvantages/ advantages?

151. Has requirements gathering uncovered information that would necessitate changes?

152. What are the acceptance criteria?

153. What is the risk associated with cost and schedule?

154. Where do system and software requirements come from, what are sources?

155. Are there legal issues?

156. What kind of entity is a problem ?

157. Is your business case still valid?

158. Is the origin of the requirement clearly stated?

159. If applicable; are there issues linked with the fact that this is an offshore Competitive Threats project?

160. Where are business rules being captured?

161. How will the proposed Competitive Threats project help?

162. Does the system provide the functions which best support the customers needs?

163. Where do you define what is a customer, what are the attributes of customer?

164. Do your constraints stand?

165. Completeness. are all functions required by the customer included?

166. What are current process problems?

167. Who is interacting with the system?

168. Can the requirement be changed without a large impact on other requirements?

2.5 Requirements Traceability Matrix: Competitive Threats

169. What are the chronologies, contingencies, consequences, criteria?

170. Why do you manage scope?

171. Describe the process for approving requirements so they can be added to the traceability matrix and Competitive Threats project work can be performed. Will the Competitive Threats project requirements become approved in writing?

172. Will you use a Requirements Traceability Matrix?

173. How will it affect the stakeholders personally in career?

174. What is the WBS?

175. How small is small enough?

176. What percentage of Competitive Threats projects are producing traceability matrices between requirements and other work products?

177. How do you manage scope?

178. Is there a requirements traceability process in place?

179. Do you have a clear understanding of all

subcontracts in place?

180. Why use a WBS?

2.6 Project Scope Statement: Competitive Threats

181. Are there specific processes you will use to evaluate and approve/reject changes?

182. If there are vendors, have they signed off on the Competitive Threats project Plan?

183. Elements of scope management that deal with concept development ?

184. What is the product of this Competitive Threats project?

185. Is this process communicated to the customer and team members?

186. Identify how your team and you will create the Competitive Threats project scope statement and the work breakdown structure (WBS). Document how you will create the Competitive Threats project scope statement and WBS, and make sure you answer the following questions: In defining Competitive Threats project scope and the WBS, will you and your Competitive Threats project team be using methods defined by your organization, methods defined by the Competitive Threats project management office (PMO), or other methods?

187. Is the change control process documented and on file?

188. Are there backup strategies for key members of the Competitive Threats project?

189. Elements that deal with providing the detail?

190. What are the major deliverables of the Competitive Threats project?

191. How will you verify the accuracy of the work of the Competitive Threats project, and what constitutes acceptance of the deliverables?

192. Any new risks introduced or old risks impacted. Are there issues that could affect the existing requirements for the result, service, or product if the scope changes?

193. What is a process you might recommend to verify the accuracy of the research deliverable?

194. Has everyone approved the Competitive Threats projects scope statement?

195. Will the Competitive Threats project risks be managed according to the Competitive Threats projects risk management process?

196. Is there a Quality Assurance Plan documented and filed?

197. Is the Competitive Threats project organization documented and on file?

198. How often will scope changes be reviewed?

199. What are the defined meeting materials?

2.7 Assumption and Constraint Log: Competitive Threats

200. Are there processes in place to ensure that all the terms and code concepts have been documented consistently?

201. Is the amount of effort justified by the anticipated value of forming a new process?

202. No superfluous information or marketing narrative?

203. What weaknesses do you have?

204. Is staff trained on the software technologies that are being used on the Competitive Threats project?

205. What worked well?

206. Does the Competitive Threats project have a formal Competitive Threats project Plan?

207. Have all stakeholders been identified?

208. Do documented requirements exist for all critical components and areas, including technical, business, interfaces, performance, security and conversion requirements?

209. Was the document/deliverable developed per the appropriate or required standards (for example, Institute of Electrical and Electronics Engineers

standards)?

210. When can log be discarded?

211. Model-building: what data-analytic strategies are useful when building proportional-hazards models?

212. What does an audit system look like?

213. How can constraints be violated?

214. Does a specific action and/or state that is known to violate security policy occur?

215. Does the system design reflect the requirements?

216. Have you eliminated all duplicative tasks or manual efforts, where appropriate?

217. Are there procedures in place to effectively manage interdependencies with other Competitive Threats projects / systems?

218. Are formal code reviews conducted?

219. Are there unnecessary steps that are creating bottlenecks and/or causing people to wait?

2.8 Work Breakdown Structure: Competitive Threats

220. Why would you develop a Work Breakdown Structure?

221. Is it still viable?

222. Why is it useful?

223. What has to be done?

224. Is it a change in scope?

225. When would you develop a Work Breakdown Structure?

226. How big is a work-package?

227. Is the work breakdown structure (wbs) defined and is the scope of the Competitive Threats project clear with assigned deliverable owners?

228. When do you stop?

229. How far down?

230. Who has to do it?

231. Where does it take place?

232. When does it have to be done?

233. How will you and your Competitive Threats project team define the Competitive Threats projects scope and work breakdown structure?

234. How much detail?

235. Do you need another level?

2.9 WBS Dictionary: Competitive Threats

236. Intermediate schedules, as required, which provide a logical sequence from the master schedule to the control account level?

237. Are the requirements for all items of overhead established by rational, traceable processes?

238. Are procedures established to prevent changes to the contract budget base other than the already stated authorized by contractual action?

239. Are estimates of costs at completion utilized in determining contract funding requirements and reporting them?

240. Is all budget available as management reserve identified and excluded from the performance measurement baseline?

241. Are retroactive changes to BCWS and BCWP prohibited except for correction of errors or for normal accounting adjustments?

242. Does the contractor require sufficient detailed planning of control accounts to constrain the application of budget initially allocated for future effort to current effort?

243. Do procedures specify under what circumstances replanning of open work packages may occur, and the

methods to be followed?

244. The anticipated business volume?

245. Are records maintained to show full accountability for all material purchased for the contract, including the residual inventory?

246. Are indirect costs charged to the appropriate indirect pools and incurring organization?

247. Are the bases and rates for allocating costs from each indirect pool to commercial work consistent with the already stated used to allocate corresponding costs to Government contracts?

248. Does the contractor use objective results, design reviews and tests to trace schedule performance?

249. Are control accounts opened and closed based on the start and completion of work contained therein?

250. Does the contractors system provide for the determination of cost variances attributable to the excess usage of material?

251. Is authorization of budgets in excess of the contract budget base controlled formally and done with the full knowledge and recognition of the procuring activity?

252. Evaluate the performance of operating organizations?

253. Are the wbs and organizational levels for

application of the Competitive Threats projected overhead costs identified?

254. Is subcontracted work defined and identified to the appropriate subcontractor within the proper WBS element?

255. Time-phased control account budgets?

2.10 Schedule Management Plan: Competitive Threats

256. Is the plan consistent with industry best practices?

257. Are target dates established for each milestone deliverable?

258. Does the resource management plan include a personnel development plan?

259. Is there an onboarding process in place?

260. Are the activity durations realistic and at an appropriate level of detail for effective management?

261. Are mitigation strategies identified?

262. Is there a procedure for management, control and release of schedule margin?

263. Is a process defined to measure the performance of the schedule management process itself?

264. Does the ims reflect accurate current status and credible start/finish forecasts for all to-go tasks and milestones?

265. Is it standard practice to formally commit stakeholders to the Competitive Threats project via agreements?

266. Competitive Threats project definition & scope?

267. Are risk triggers captured?

268. Why time management?

269. Is your organization certified as a supplier, wholesaler and/or regular dealer?

270. Has the business need been clearly defined?

271. What tools and techniques will be used to estimate activity durations?

272. Are action items captured and managed?

273. Do Competitive Threats project teams & team members report on status / activities / progress?

2.11 Activity List: Competitive Threats

274. What is the total time required to complete the Competitive Threats project if no delays occur?

275. What is the probability the Competitive Threats project can be completed in xx weeks?

276. When do the individual activities need to start and finish?

277. How will it be performed?

278. In what sequence?

279. Can you determine the activity that must finish, before this activity can start?

280. What did not go as well?

281. How difficult will it be to do specific activities on this Competitive Threats project?

282. How do you determine the late start (LS) for each activity?

283. When will the work be performed?

284. Is there anything planned that does not need to be here?

285. What are you counting on?

286. Are the required resources available or need to

be acquired?

287. How much slack is available in the Competitive Threats project?

288. What is your organizations history in doing similar activities?

289. What is the LF and LS for each activity?

290. The wbs is developed as part of a joint planning session. and how do you know that youhave done this right?

291. How detailed should a Competitive Threats project get?

292. Should you include sub-activities?

2.12 Activity Attributes: Competitive Threats

293. Does your organization of the data change its meaning?

294. Time for overtime?

295. Has management defined a definite timeframe for the turnaround or Competitive Threats project window?

296. Where else does it apply?

297. Resources to accomplish the work?

298. Have constraints been applied to the start and finish milestones for the phases?

299. Would you consider either of corresponding activities an outlier?

300. How much activity detail is required?

301. Activity: what is In the Bag?

302. What activity do you think you should spend the most time on?

303. Do you feel very comfortable with your prediction?

304. Were there other ways you could have organized

the data to achieve similar results?

305. How many days do you need to complete the work scope with a limit of X number of resources?

306. Are the required resources available?

307. What went wrong?

308. What is the general pattern here?

309. How difficult will it be to do specific activities on this Competitive Threats project?

2.13 Milestone List: Competitive Threats

310. How difficult will it be to do specific activities on this Competitive Threats project?

311. How soon can the activity start?

312. How will you get the word out to customers?

313. Continuity, supply chain robustness?

314. Global influences?

315. What background experience, skills, and strengths does the team bring to your organization?

316. Who will manage the Competitive Threats project on a day-to-day basis?

317. Reliability of data, plan predictability?

318. Usps (unique selling points)?

319. How will the milestone be verified?

320. Calculate how long can activity be delayed?

321. Obstacles faced?

322. Own known vulnerabilities?

323. Timescales, deadlines and pressures?

324. Level of the Innovation?

325. It is to be a narrative text providing the crucial aspects of your Competitive Threats project proposal answering what, who, how, when and where?

326. Environmental effects?

327. Which path is the critical path?

328. Describe the concept of the technology, product or service that will be or has been developed. How will it be used?

2.14 Network Diagram: Competitive Threats

329. If x is long, what would be the completion time if you break x into two parallel parts of y weeks and z weeks?

330. What can be done concurrently?

331. Review the logical flow of the network diagram. Take a look at which activities you have first and then sequence the activities. Do they make sense?

332. What job or jobs could run concurrently?

333. Where do you schedule uncertainty time?

334. What to do and When?

335. What controls the start and finish of a job?

336. Are the gantt chart and/or network diagram updated periodically and used to assess the overall Competitive Threats project timetable?

337. How difficult will it be to do specific activities on this Competitive Threats project?

338. What job or jobs follow it?

339. Will crashing x weeks return more in benefits than it costs?

340. Are you on time?

341. Exercise: what is the probability that the Competitive Threats project duration will exceed xx weeks?

342. What activities must follow this activity?

343. What is the probability of completing the Competitive Threats project in less that xx days?

344. What are the tools?

345. Planning: who, how long, what to do?

346. What activity must be completed immediately before this activity can start?

2.15 Activity Resource Requirements: Competitive Threats

347. How many signatures do you require on a check and does this match what is in your policy and procedures?

348. Do you use tools like decomposition and rolling-wave planning to produce the activity list and other outputs?

349. Are there unresolved issues that need to be addressed?

350. What is the Work Plan Standard?

351. Other support in specific areas?

352. How do you handle petty cash?

353. Anything else?

354. Which logical relationship does the PDM use most often?

355. What are constraints that you might find during the Human Resource Planning process?

356. Why do you do that?

357. When does monitoring begin?

2.16 Resource Breakdown Structure: Competitive Threats

358. What defines a successful Competitive Threats project?

359. Who needs what information?

360. Which resource planning tool provides information on resource responsibility and accountability?

361. Who is allowed to see what data about which resources?

362. Why is this important?

363. What is the number one predictor of a groups productivity?

364. What defines a successful Competitive Threats project?

365. What can you do to improve productivity?

366. When do they need the information?

367. Goals for the Competitive Threats project. What is each stakeholders desired outcome for the Competitive Threats project?

368. What is the purpose of assigning and documenting responsibility?

369. Changes based on input from stakeholders?

370. What is the difference between % Complete and % work?

371. How can this help you with team building?

372. Who is allowed to perform which functions?

2.17 Activity Duration Estimates: Competitive Threats

373. (Cpi), and schedule performance index (spi) for the Competitive Threats project?

374. Do you think Competitive Threats project managers of large information technology Competitive Threats projects need strong technical skills?

375. Total slack can be calculated by which equations?

376. Are processes defined to monitor Competitive Threats project cost and schedule variances?

377. What is the career outlook for Competitive Threats project managers in information technology?

378. How can organizations use a weighted decision matrix to evaluate proposals as part of source selection?

379. Do an internet search on earning pmp certification. be sure to search for yahoo groups related to this topic. what are the options you found to help people prepare for the exam?

380. Which is the BEST Competitive Threats project management tool to use to determine the longest time the Competitive Threats project will take?

381. Are performance reviews conducted regularly to

assess the status of Competitive Threats projects?

382. Is a Competitive Threats project charter created once a Competitive Threats project is formally recognized?

383. When would a milestone chart be used instead of a bar char?

384. Consider the common sources of risk on information technology Competitive Threats projects and suggestions for managing them. Which suggestions do you find most useful?

385. Is training acquired to enhance the skills, knowledge and capabilities of the Competitive Threats project team?

386. Does a process exist for approving or rejecting changes?

387. Does a process exist to identify Competitive Threats project roles, responsibilities and reporting relationships?

388. Are risks monitored to determine if an event has occurred or if the mitigation was successful?

389. What does it mean to take a systems view of a Competitive Threats project?

390. Are costs that may be needed to account for Competitive Threats project risks determined?

2.18 Duration Estimating Worksheet: Competitive Threats

391. Is this operation cost effective?

392. What is cost and Competitive Threats project cost management?

393. How can the Competitive Threats project be displayed graphically to better visualize the activities?

394. Will the Competitive Threats project collaborate with the local community and leverage resources?

395. What utility impacts are there?

396. Value pocket identification & quantification what are value pockets?

397. For other activities, how much delay can be tolerated?

398. What is the total time required to complete the Competitive Threats project if no delays occur?

399. Science = process: remember the scientific method?

400. When does your organization expect to be able to complete it?

401. How should ongoing costs be monitored to try to keep the Competitive Threats project within budget?

402. What is next?

403. What are the critical bottleneck activities?

404. Define the work as completely as possible. What work will be included in the Competitive Threats project?

405. What questions do you have?

406. Why estimate time and cost?

407. Is a construction detail attached (to aid in explanation)?

408. Small or large Competitive Threats project?

2.19 Project Schedule: Competitive Threats

409. Why is software Competitive Threats project disaster so common?

410. Does the condition or event threaten the Competitive Threats projects objectives in any ways?

411. Have all Competitive Threats project delays been adequately accounted for, communicated to all stakeholders and adjustments made in overall Competitive Threats project schedule?

412. What does that mean?

413. How many levels?

414. Did the Competitive Threats project come in on schedule?

415. Are all remaining durations correct?

416. Verify that the update is accurate. Are all remaining durations correct?

417. If you can not fix it, how do you do it differently?

418. How can you minimize or control changes to Competitive Threats project schedules?

419. Understand the constraints used in preparing the schedule. Are activities connected because logic

dictates the order in which others occur?

420. How can you address that situation?

421. It allows the Competitive Threats project to be delivered on schedule. How Do you Use Schedules?

422. Why do you need schedules?

423. Are quality inspections and review activities listed in the Competitive Threats project schedule(s)?

424. How detailed should a Competitive Threats project get?

425. Are procedures defined by which the Competitive Threats project schedule may be changed?

426. Did the Competitive Threats project come in under budget?

2.20 Cost Management Plan: Competitive Threats

427. Have activity relationships and interdependencies within tasks been adequately identified?

428. Schedule variances – how will schedule variances be identified and corrected?

429. Have the reasons why the changes to your organizational systems and capabilities are required?

430. Are tasks tracked by hours?

431. Has the Competitive Threats project scope been baselined?

432. Have the key functions and capabilities been defined and assigned to each release or iteration?

433. Are schedule deliverables actually delivered?

434. Is current scope of the Competitive Threats project substantially different than that originally defined?

435. Is Competitive Threats project status reviewed with the steering and executive teams at appropriate intervals?

436. Time management – how will the schedule impact of changes be estimated and approved?

437. Schedule contingency – how will the schedule contingency be administrated?

438. Escalation criteria met?

439. Was the Competitive Threats project schedule reviewed by all stakeholders and formally accepted?

440. Does the detailed work plan match the complexity of tasks with the capabilities of personnel?

441. Change types and category – What are the types of changes and what are the techniques to report and control changes?

442. Are there checklists created to determine if all quality processes are followed?

443. Pareto diagrams, statistical sampling, flow charting or trend analysis used quality monitoring?

444. Designated small business reserve?

445. Is there a requirements change management processes in place?

2.21 Activity Cost Estimates: Competitive Threats

446. How do you allocate indirect costs to activities?

447. Were you satisfied with the work?

448. Where can you get activity reports?

449. Were the tasks or work products prepared by the consultant useful?

450. Were sponsors and decision makers available when needed outside regularly scheduled meetings?

451. Will you need to provide essential services information about activities?

452. How and when do you enter into Competitive Threats project Procurement Management?

453. What is the estimators estimating history?

454. What is included in indirect cost being allocated?

455. How quickly can the task be done with the skills available?

456. How do you change activities?

457. What skill level is required to do the job?

458. Will you use any tools, such as Competitive

Threats project management software, to assist in capturing Earned Value metrics?

459. Did the Competitive Threats project team have the right skills?

460. Who determines when the contractor is paid?

461. Were escalated issues resolved promptly?

462. Are cost subtotals needed?

463. Were the costs or charges reasonable?

2.22 Cost Estimating Worksheet: Competitive Threats

464. What is the estimated labor cost today based upon this information?

465. What costs are to be estimated?

466. What is the purpose of estimating?

467. Who is best positioned to know and assist in identifying corresponding factors?

468. What can be included?

469. What info is needed?

470. Ask: are others positioned to know, are others credible, and will others cooperate?

471. Does the Competitive Threats project provide innovative ways for stakeholders to overcome obstacles or deliver better outcomes?

472. How will the results be shared and to whom?

473. Is it feasible to establish a control group arrangement?

474. Will the Competitive Threats project collaborate with the local community and leverage resources?

475. What additional Competitive Threats project(s)

could be initiated as a result of this Competitive Threats project?

476. Is the Competitive Threats project responsive to community need?

477. What will others want?

478. Can a trend be established from historical performance data on the selected measure and are the criteria for using trend analysis or forecasting methods met?

479. Identify the timeframe necessary to monitor progress and collect data to determine how the selected measure has changed?

480. What happens to any remaining funds not used?

2.23 Cost Baseline: Competitive Threats

481. Are you meeting with your team regularly?

482. Is there anything you need from upper management in order to be successful?

483. What do you want to measure ?

484. What strengths do you have?

485. How will cost estimates be used?

486. Does the suggested change request seem to represent a necessary enhancement to the product?

487. At which frequency ?

488. Are procedures defined by which the cost baseline may be changed?

489. What is your organizations history in doing similar tasks?

490. Is there anything unique in this Competitive Threats projects scope statement that will affect resources?

491. Who will use corresponding metrics ?

492. How fast?

493. Has the documentation relating to operation and maintenance of the product(s) or service(s) been delivered to, and accepted by, operations management?

494. If you sold 10x widgets on a day, what would the affect on profits be?

495. Should a more thorough impact analysis be conducted?

496. Is the requested change request a result of changes in other Competitive Threats project(s)?

497. Definition of done can be traced back to the definitions of what are you providing to the customer in terms of deliverables?

498. What deliverables come first?

499. Has the Competitive Threats projected annual cost to operate and maintain the product(s) or service(s) been approved and funded?

2.24 Quality Management Plan: Competitive Threats

500. Results Available?

501. What is the audience for the data?

502. Can it be done better?

503. How do you decide what information needs to be recorded?

504. Sampling part of task?

505. How relevant is this attribute to this Competitive Threats project or audit?

506. How does your organization maintain a safe and healthy work environment?

507. Does the Competitive Threats project have a formal Competitive Threats project Plan?

508. How effectively was the Quality Management Plan applied during Competitive Threats project Execution?

509. Contradictory information between document sections?

510. What are your organizations current levels and trends for the already stated measures related to financial and marketplace performance?

511. How do you decide what information to record?

512. Does a documented Competitive Threats project organizational policy & plan (i.e. governance model) exist?

513. Are best practices and metrics employed to identify issues, progress, performance, etc.?

514. How are changes to procedures made?

515. What are your organizations current levels and trends for the already stated measures related to customer satisfaction/ dissatisfaction and product/ service performance?

516. Was trending evident between audits?

517. Are there trends or hot spots?

518. If it is out of compliance, should the process be amended or should the Plan be amended?

519. What is the Quality Management Plan?

2.25 Quality Metrics: Competitive Threats

520. Have risk areas been identified?

521. Were number of defects identified?

522. Is there alignment within your organization on definitions?

523. How do you know if everyone is trying to improve the right things?

524. Did evaluation start on time?

525. When will the Final Guidance will be issued?

526. What are your organizations next steps?

527. Is the reporting frequency appropriate?

528. Has trace of defects been initiated?

529. What happens if you get an abnormal result?

530. Are documents on hand to provide explanations of privacy and confidentiality?

531. What percentage are outcome-based?

532. What forces exist that would cause them to change?

533. How does one achieve stability?

534. If the defect rate during testing is substantially higher than that of the previous release (or a similar product), then ask: Did you plan for and actually improve testing effectiveness?

535. How do you calculate such metrics?

536. Was material distributed on time?

537. What is the timeline to meet your goal?

538. Was the overall quality better or worse than previous products?

539. Where did complaints, returns and warranty claims come from?

2.26 Process Improvement Plan: Competitive Threats

540. Has a process guide to collect the data been developed?

541. What is the test-cycle concept?

542. Are you making progress on your improvement plan?

543. What makes people good SPI coaches?

544. Why do you want to achieve the goal?

545. What lessons have you learned so far?

546. Have the supporting tools been developed or acquired?

547. Management commitment at all levels?

548. Are you making progress on the goals?

549. What personnel are the sponsors for that initiative?

550. How do you manage quality?

551. Have the frequency of collection and the points in the process where measurements will be made been determined?

552. Who should prepare the process improvement action plan?

553. Are you following the quality standards?

554. Are you meeting the quality standards?

555. What personnel are the champions for the initiative?

556. Does your process ensure quality?

557. What actions are needed to address the problems and achieve the goals?

558. To elicit goal statements, do you ask a question such as, What do you want to achieve?

2.27 Responsibility Assignment Matrix: Competitive Threats

559. What materials and procurements needed?

560. Are indirect costs accumulated for comparison with the corresponding budgets?

561. Will too many Communicating responsibilities tangle the Competitive Threats project in unnecessary communications?

562. Are all elements of indirect expense identified to overhead cost budgets of Competitive Threats projections?

563. Undistributed budgets, if any?

564. Authorization to proceed with all authorized work?

565. Too many as: does a proper segregation of duties exist?

566. What will the work cost?

567. What are the assumptions?

568. Is data disseminated to the contractors management timely, accurate, and usable?

569. Do work packages consist of discrete tasks which are adequately described?

570. Cwbs elements to be subcontracted, with identification of subcontractors?

571. Is the entire contract planned in time-phased control accounts to the extent practicable?

572. Detailed schedules which support control account and work package start and completion dates/events?

573. Why cost benefit analysis?

574. No rs: if a task has no one listed as responsible, who is getting the job done?

575. Availability – will the group or the person be available within the necessary time interval?

2.28 Roles and Responsibilities: Competitive Threats

576. Authority: what areas/Competitive Threats projects in your work do you have the authority to decide upon and act on the already stated decisions?

577. Does your vision/mission support a culture of quality data?

578. Where are you most strong as a supervisor?

579. Are your budgets supportive of a culture of quality data?

580. Are governance roles and responsibilities documented?

581. Who is responsible for implementation activities and where will the functions, roles and responsibilities be defined?

582. Do you take the time to clearly define roles and responsibilities on Competitive Threats project tasks?

583. What are your major roles and responsibilities in the area of performance measurement and assessment?

584. Be specific; avoid generalities. Thank you and great work alone are insufficient. What exactly do you appreciate and why?

585. What should you highlight for improvement?

586. Once the responsibilities are defined for the Competitive Threats project, have the deliverables, roles and responsibilities been clearly communicated to every participant?

587. What areas would you highlight for changes or improvements?

588. Accountabilities: what are the roles and responsibilities of individual team members?

589. Does the team have access to and ability to use data analysis tools?

590. To decide whether to use a quality measurement, ask how will you know when it is achieved?

591. Are Competitive Threats project team roles and responsibilities identified and documented?

592. Is the data complete?

593. How is your work-life balance?

594. Is there a training program in place for stakeholders covering expectations, roles and responsibilities and any addition knowledge others need to be good stakeholders?

595. What expectations were NOT met?

2.29 Human Resource Management Plan: Competitive Threats

596. Is quality monitored from the perspective of the customers needs and expectations?

597. Is there an issues management plan in place?

598. Is pert / critical path or equivalent methodology being used?

599. How are superior performers differentiated from average performers?

600. What is the boss?

601. Was the scope definition used in task sequencing?

602. Were Competitive Threats project team members involved in detailed estimating and scheduling?

603. Are the Competitive Threats project team members located locally to the users/stakeholders?

604. Have all team members been part of identifying risks?

605. Are adequate resources provided for the quality assurance function?

606. Staffing Requirements?

607. What are the Staffing Requirements?

608. Quality of people required to meet the forecast needs of the department?

609. Responsiveness to change and the resulting demands for different skills and abilities?

610. Have all involved Competitive Threats project stakeholders and work groups committed to the Competitive Threats project?

611. How does the proposed individual meet each requirement?

612. Has a Competitive Threats project Communications Plan been developed?

613. Competitive Threats project Objectives?

614. What is this Competitive Threats project aiming to achieve?

2.30 Communications Management Plan: Competitive Threats

615. What is Competitive Threats project communications management?

616. Which team member will work with each stakeholder?

617. How is this initiative related to other portfolios, programs, or Competitive Threats projects?

618. What is the political influence?

619. Are you constantly rushing from meeting to meeting?

620. What are the interrelationships?

621. Who have you worked with in past, similar initiatives?

622. How do you manage communications?

623. Are there potential barriers between the team and the stakeholder?

624. Who needs to know and how much?

625. Do you feel more overwhelmed by stakeholders?

626. What communications method?

627. Is the stakeholder role recognized by your organization?

628. What is the stakeholders level of authority?

629. Timing: when do the effects of the communication take place?

630. What to learn?

631. Which stakeholders can influence others?

632. What approaches to you feel are the best ones to use?

633. Why do you manage communications?

2.31 Risk Management Plan: Competitive Threats

634. Are testing tools available and suitable?

635. People risk -are people with appropriate skills available to help complete the Competitive Threats project?

636. Risk documentation: what reporting formats and processes will be used for risk management activities?

637. What is the impact to the Competitive Threats project if the item is not resolved in a timely fashion?

638. Are requirements fully understood by the software engineering team and customers?

639. Do requirements demand the use of new analysis, design, or testing methods?

640. Are team members trained in the use of the tools?

641. Financial risk -can your organization afford to undertake the Competitive Threats project?

642. Are people attending meetings and doing work?

643. How do you manage Competitive Threats project Risk?

644. Which risks should get the attention?

645. Have you worked with the customer in the past?

646. How would you suggest monitoring for risk transition indicators?

647. Are the best people available?

648. User involvement: do you have the right users?

649. What will the damage be?

650. Are the reports useful and easy to read?

651. Prioritized components/features?

652. Does the customer understand the software process?

2.32 Risk Register: Competitive Threats

653. How are risks graded?

654. What evidence do you have to justify the likelihood score of the risk (audit, incident report, claim, complaints, inspection, internal review)?

655. What are your key risks/show istoppers and what is being done to manage them?

656. What would the impact to the Competitive Threats project objectives be should the risk arise?

657. Preventative actions - planned actions to reduce the likelihood a risk will occur and/or reduce the seriousness should it occur. What should you do now?

658. Does the evidence highlight any areas to advance opportunities or foster good relations. If yes what steps will be taken?

659. People risk -are people with appropriate skills available to help complete the Competitive Threats project?

660. Are your objectives at risk?

661. What is your current and future risk profile?

662. Contingency actions - planned actions to reduce the immediate seriousness of the risk when it does

occur. What should you do when?

663. What is a Risk?

664. Schedule impact/severity estimated range (workdays) assume the event happens, what is the potential impact?

665. Who needs to know about this?

666. Amongst the action plans and recommendations that you have to introduce are there some that could stop or delay the overall program?

667. When would you develop a risk register?

668. Which key risks have ineffective responses or outstanding improvement actions?

669. Methodology: how will risk management be performed on this Competitive Threats project?

670. Can the likelihood and impact of failing to achieve corresponding recommendations and action plans be assessed?

671. What should you do now?

2.33 Probability and Impact Assessment: Competitive Threats

672. Who will be responsible for a slippage?

673. Are the facilities, expertise, resources, and management know-how available to handle the situation?

674. Are the risk data complete?

675. How completely has the customer been identified?

676. Does the Competitive Threats project team have experience with the technology to be implemented?

677. Is a software Competitive Threats project management tool available?

678. Are tool mentors available?

679. Does the software engineering team have the right mix of skills?

680. What is the likelihood of a breakthrough?

681. What is the risk appetite?

682. Can the risk be avoided by choosing a different alternative?

683. Can the Competitive Threats project proceed

without assuming the risk?

684. Are some people working on multiple Competitive Threats projects?

685. Costs associated with late delivery or a defective product?

686. Does the software interface with new or unproven hardware or unproven vendor products?

687. What is the level of experience available with your organization?

2.34 Probability and Impact Matrix: Competitive Threats

688. What will be the environmental impact of the Competitive Threats project?

689. Which of the risk factors can be avoided altogether?

690. What new technologies are being explored in the same area?

691. What are the chances the risk events will occur?

692. Are there alternative opinions/solutions/ processes you should explore?

693. What would be the best solution?

694. What would you do differently?

695. Sensitivity analysis -which risks will have the most impact on the Competitive Threats project?

696. What should you do FIRST?

697. Which is the BEST thing to do?

698. What risks are necessary to achieve success?

699. What will be cost of redeployment of the personnel?

700. How will the consumption pattern change?

701. Were there any Competitive Threats projects similar to this one in existence?

702. How to prioritize risks?

703. What is Competitive Threats project risk management?

2.35 Risk Data Sheet: Competitive Threats

704. Type of risk identified?

705. If it happens, what are the consequences?

706. What are the main opportunities available to you that you should grab while you can?

707. How reliable is the data source?

708. What are your core values?

709. What actions can be taken to eliminate or remove risk?

710. What can you do?

711. What if client refuses?

712. How do you handle product safely?

713. What are you weak at and therefore need to do better?

714. What are you trying to achieve (Objectives)?

715. Whom do you serve (customers)?

716. Potential for recurrence?

717. Risk of what?

718. Is the data sufficiently specified in terms of the type of failure being analyzed, and its frequency or probability?

719. During work activities could hazards exist?

720. Has a sensitivity analysis been carried out?

721. What do people affected think about the need for, and practicality of preventive measures?

722. Will revised controls lead to tolerable risk levels?

2.36 Procurement Management Plan: Competitive Threats

723. Is the assigned Competitive Threats project manager a PMP (Certified Competitive Threats project manager) and experienced?

724. Has the schedule been baselined?

725. Is there general agreement & acceptance of the current status and progress of the Competitive Threats project?

726. Are key risk mitigation strategies added to the Competitive Threats project schedule?

727. Is the steering committee active in Competitive Threats project oversight?

728. Specific - is the objective clear in terms of what, how, when, and where the situation will be changed?

729. Are all key components of a Quality Assurance Plan present?

730. What areas does the group agree are the biggest success on the Competitive Threats project?

731. Are the payment terms being followed?

732. Has a quality assurance plan been developed for the Competitive Threats project?

733. Is the communication plan being followed?

734. Are vendor contract reports, reviews and visits conducted periodically?

735. Has the Competitive Threats project scope been baselined?

736. Have all involved Competitive Threats project stakeholders and work groups committed to the Competitive Threats project?

737. What is the last item a Competitive Threats project manager must do to finalize Competitive Threats project close-out?

2.37 Source Selection Criteria: Competitive Threats

738. What should clarifications include?

739. What will you use to capture evaluation and subsequent documentation?

740. Can you prevent comparison of proposals?

741. Are considerations anticipated?

742. When is it appropriate to issue a Draft Request for Proposal (DRFP)?

743. Have team members been adequately trained?

744. How important is cost in the source selection decision relative to past performance and technical considerations?

745. What benefits are accrued from issuing a DRFP in advance of issuing a final RFP?

746. Is experience evaluated?

747. What are open book debriefings?

748. Is a cost realism analysis used?

749. What is price analysis and when should it be performed?

750. How should oral presentations be prepared for?

751. Do you want to have them collaborate at subfactor level?

752. Who is entitled to a debriefing?

753. How can business terms and conditions be improved to yield more effective price competition?

754. How do you facilitate evaluation against published criteria?

755. What information is to be provided and when should it be provided?

756. Does your documentation identify why the team concurs or differs with reported performance from past performance report (CPARs, questionnaire responses, etc.)?

2.38 Stakeholder Management Plan: Competitive Threats

757. Are metrics used to evaluate and manage Vendors?

758. Are internal Competitive Threats project status meetings held at reasonable intervals?

759. Have Competitive Threats project management standards and procedures been established and documented?

760. Where are the verification requirements to be documented (eg purchase order, agreement etc)?

761. What inspection and testing is to be performed?

762. Describe the process that will be used to design, develop, review, accept, distribute and change outputs. Will all outputs delivered by the Competitive Threats project follow the same process?

763. Do Competitive Threats project teams & team members report on status / activities / progress?

764. Are updated Competitive Threats project time & resource estimates reasonable based on the current Competitive Threats project stage?

765. Does the Competitive Threats project have a formal Competitive Threats project Charter?

766. Are Competitive Threats project team members involved in detailed estimating and scheduling?

767. Does a documented Competitive Threats project organizational policy & plan (i.e. governance model) exist?

768. Does the Competitive Threats project have a Quality Culture?

769. What are the procedures and processes to be followed for purchases, including approval and authorisation requirements?

770. Is the performance of the supplier to be rated and documented?

771. Is there general agreement & acceptance of the current status and progress of the Competitive Threats project?

2.39 Change Management Plan: Competitive Threats

772. How badly can information be misinterpreted?

773. How do you know the requirements you documented are the right ones?

774. Is there an adequate supply of people for the new roles?

775. What are you trying to achieve as a result of communication?

776. Will all field readiness criteria have been practically met prior to training roll-out?

777. Clearly articulate the overall business benefits of the Competitive Threats project -why are you doing this now?

778. Are there resource implications for your communications strategy?

779. What risks may occur upfront?

780. How much change management is needed?

781. Where do you want to be?

782. How far reaching in your organization is the change?

783. Are work location changes required?

784. Is there a support model for this application and are the details available for distribution?

785. What type of materials/channels will be available to leverage?

786. Has the training co-ordinator been provided with the training details and put in place the necessary arrangements?

787. What is the most positive interpretation it can receive?

788. When does it make sense to customize?

789. Do the proposed users have access to the appropriate documentation?

790. What skills, education, knowledge, or work experiences should the resources have for each identified competency?

3.0 Executing Process Group: Competitive Threats

791. How well did the chosen processes produce the expected results?

792. Will outside resources be needed to help?

793. Could a new application negatively affect the current IT infrastructure?

794. Will a new application be developed using existing hardware, software, and networks?

795. How do you measure difficulty?

796. What are the main types of goods and services being outsourced?

797. Is the Competitive Threats project making progress in helping to achieve the set results?

798. What are the Competitive Threats project management deliverables of each process group?

799. What are deliverables of your Competitive Threats project?

800. What are the typical Competitive Threats project management skills?

801. It under budget or over budget?

802. Is activity definition the first process involved in Competitive Threats project time management?

803. What were things that you did very well and want to do the same again on the next Competitive Threats project?

804. On which process should team members spend the most time?

805. In what way has the program come up with innovative measures for problem-solving?

806. What are the main types of contracts if you do decide to outsource?

807. What type of information goes in the quality assurance plan?

808. How do you enter durations, link tasks, and view critical path information?

809. What are crucial elements of successful Competitive Threats project plan execution?

3.1 Team Member Status Report: Competitive Threats

810. How can you make it practical?

811. Why is it to be done?

812. Is there evidence that staff is taking a more professional approach toward management of your organizations Competitive Threats projects?

813. Does your organization have the means (staff, money, contract, etc.) to produce or to acquire the product, good, or service?

814. When a teams productivity and success depend on collaboration and the efficient flow of information, what generally fails them?

815. What specific interest groups do you have in place?

816. Does the product, good, or service already exist within your organization?

817. The problem with Reward & Recognition Programs is that the truly deserving people all too often get left out. How can you make it practical?

818. Does every department have to have a Competitive Threats project Manager on staff?

819. How does this product, good, or service meet the

needs of the Competitive Threats project and your organization as a whole?

820. Are the products of your organizations Competitive Threats projects meeting customers objectives?

821. Are your organizations Competitive Threats projects more successful over time?

822. How much risk is involved?

823. What is to be done?

824. Do you have an Enterprise Competitive Threats project Management Office (EPMO)?

825. How it is to be done?

826. Are the attitudes of staff regarding Competitive Threats project work improving?

827. How will resource planning be done?

828. Will the staff do training or is that done by a third party?

3.2 Change Request: Competitive Threats

829. Who can suggest changes?

830. Who will perform the change?

831. How many times must the change be modified or presented to the change control board before it is approved?

832. Can static requirements change attributes like the size of the change be used to predict reliability in execution?

833. How can changes be graded?

834. Is it feasible to use requirements attributes as predictors of reliability?

835. What type of changes does change control take into account?

836. Why were your requested changes rejected or not made?

837. Will this change conflict with other requirements changes (e.g., lead to conflicting operational scenarios)?

838. Who is included in the change control team?

839. How fast will change requests be approved?

840. How can you ensure that changes have been made properly?

841. How is the change documented (format, content, storage)?

842. Screen shots or attachments included in a Change Request?

843. What kind of information about the change request needs to be captured?

844. What is the relationship between requirements attributes and reliability?

845. Who needs to approve change requests?

846. Why do you want to have a change control system?

847. When do you create a change request?

848. What needs to be communicated?

3.3 Change Log: Competitive Threats

849. How does this relate to the standards developed for specific business processes?

850. Is the change request within Competitive Threats project scope?

851. Where do changes come from?

852. Does the suggested change request represent a desired enhancement to the products functionality?

853. Who initiated the change request?

854. Is this a mandatory replacement?

855. How does this change affect scope?

856. Is the change backward compatible without limitations?

857. How does this change affect the timeline of the schedule?

858. Will the Competitive Threats project fail if the change request is not executed?

859. Is the submitted change a new change or a modification of a previously approved change?

860. Is the requested change request a result of changes in other Competitive Threats project(s)?

861. When was the request submitted?

862. When was the request approved?

863. Is the change request open, closed or pending?

864. Do the described changes impact on the integrity or security of the system?

3.4 Decision Log: Competitive Threats

865. How effective is maintaining the log at facilitating organizational learning?

866. What makes you different or better than others companies selling the same thing?

867. How do you know when you are achieving it?

868. Adversarial environment. is your opponent open to a non-traditional workflow, or will it likely challenge anything you do?

869. At what point in time does loss become unacceptable?

870. Is everything working as expected?

871. Does anything need to be adjusted?

872. It becomes critical to track and periodically revisit both operational effectiveness; Are you noticing all that you need to, and are you interpreting what you see effectively?

873. How do you define success?

874. Linked to original objective?

875. How consolidated and comprehensive a story can you tell by capturing currently available incident data in a central location and through a log of key decisions during an incident?

876. Is your opponent open to a non-traditional workflow, or will it likely challenge anything you do?

877. Who will be given a copy of this document and where will it be kept?

878. Which variables make a critical difference?

879. Do strategies and tactics aimed at less than full control reduce the costs of management or simply shift the cost burden?

880. What was the rationale for the decision?

881. How does the use a Decision Support System influence the strategies/tactics or costs?

882. What eDiscovery problem or issue did your organization set out to fix or make better?

883. How does provision of information, both in terms of content and presentation, influence acceptance of alternative strategies?

884. What are the cost implications?

3.5 Quality Audit: Competitive Threats

885. Does the report read coherently?

886. What experience do staff have in the type of work that the audit entails?

887. How does your organization know that its Mission, Vision and Values Statements are appropriate and effectively guiding your organization?

888. Are the policies and processes, as set out in the Quality Audit Manual, properly applied?

889. What is your organizations greatest strength?

890. Is the continuing professional education of key personnel account fored in detail?

891. How does your organization know that its Strategic Plan is providing the best guidance for the future of your organization?

892. Has a written procedure been established to identify devices during all stages of receipt, reconditioning, distribution and installation so that mix-ups are prevented?

893. How does your organization know that its research programs are appropriately effective and constructive?

894. Are adequate and conveniently located toilet facilities available for use by the employees?

895. How does your organization know that its quality of teaching is appropriately effective and constructive?

896. How do you know what, specifically, is required of you in your work?

897. How does your organization know that the support for its staff is appropriately effective and constructive?

898. Are goals well supported with strategies, operational plans, manuals and training?

899. How does your organization know that its systems for assisting staff with career planning and employment placements are appropriately effective and constructive?

900. How does your organization know that its relationships with industry and employers are appropriately effective and constructive?

901. Are all staff empowered and encouraged to contribute to ongoing improvement efforts?

902. How does your organization know that its system for inducting new staff to maximize workplace contributions are appropriately effective and constructive?

903. Does the suppliers quality system have a written procedure for corrective action when a defect occurs?

904. How does your organization know that its system for managing intellectual property issues is appropriately effective, constructive and fair?

3.6 Team Directory: Competitive Threats

905. Process decisions: are all start-up, turn over and close out requirements of the contract satisfied?

906. Process decisions: are contractors adequately prosecuting the work?

907. Process decisions: which organizational elements and which individuals will be assigned management functions?

908. Decisions: what could be done better to improve the quality of the constructed product?

909. Process decisions: is work progressing on schedule and per contract requirements?

910. Who should receive information (all stakeholders)?

911. Timing: when do the effects of communication take place?

912. Who is the Sponsor?

913. Process decisions: are there any statutory or regulatory issues relevant to the timely execution of work?

914. Who are the Team Members?

915. What are you going to deliver or accomplish?

916. Who will report Competitive Threats project status to all stakeholders?

917. How does the team resolve conflicts and ensure tasks are completed?

918. How do unidentified risks impact the outcome of the Competitive Threats project?

919. Do purchase specifications and configurations match requirements?

920. Process decisions: do invoice amounts match accepted work in place?

921. Days from the time the issue is identified?

922. When does information need to be distributed?

923. Decisions: is the most suitable form of contract being used?

3.7 Team Operating Agreement: Competitive Threats

924. Do you record meetings for the already stated unable to attend?

925. Do team members reside in more than two countries?

926. Confidentiality: how will confidential information be handled?

927. Seconds for members to respond?

928. Do you use a parking lot for any items that are important and outside of the agenda?

929. What is the number of cases currently teamed?

930. How does teaming fit in with overall organizational goals and meet organizational needs?

931. Do you ensure that all participants know how to use the required technology?

932. Do you post meeting notes and the recording (if used) and notify participants?

933. What resources can be provided for the team in terms of equipment, space, time for training, protected time and space for meetings, and travel allowances?

934. Do you determine the meeting length and time of day?

935. Are there differences in access to communication and collaboration technology based on team member location?

936. Have you set the goals and objectives of the team?

937. Must your team members rely on the expertise of other members to complete tasks?

938. Why does your organization want to participate in teaming?

939. Communication protocols: how will the team communicate?

940. How will you divide work equitably?

941. Do you upload presentation materials in advance and test the technology?

942. Do you brief absent members after they view meeting notes or listen to a recording?

943. Are there more than two native languages represented by your team?

3.8 Team Performance Assessment: Competitive Threats

944. How do you manage human resources?

945. Can familiarity breed backup?

946. To what degree does the teams work approach provide opportunity for members to engage in results-based evaluation?

947. How hard do you try to make a good selection?

948. To what degree do all members feel responsible for all agreed-upon measures?

949. To what degree is there a sense that only the team can succeed?

950. To what degree does the team possess adequate membership to achieve its ends?

951. To what degree are the relative importance and priority of the goals clear to all team members?

952. To what degree does the teams purpose constitute a broader, deeper aspiration than just accomplishing short-term goals?

953. Individual task proficiency and team process behavior: what is important for team functioning?

954. To what degree can team members frequently

and easily communicate with one another?

955. To what degree do members understand and articulate the same purpose without relying on ambiguous abstractions?

956. To what degree do team members feel that the purpose of the team is important, if not exciting?

957. Effects of crew composition on crew performance: Does the whole equal the sum of its parts?

958. When does the medium matter?

959. To what degree can all members engage in open and interactive considerations?

960. What makes opportunities more or less obvious?

961. If you are worried about method variance before you collect data, what sort of design elements might you include to reduce or eliminate the threat of method variance?

962. How do you recognize and praise members for contributions?

963. To what degree can the team measure progress against specific goals?

3.9 Team Member Performance Assessment: Competitive Threats

964. Is there reluctance to join a team?

965. To what degree is the team cognizant of small wins to be celebrated along the way?

966. What are they responsible for?

967. What evaluation results do you have?

968. Are the goals SMART ?

969. What, if any, steps are available for employees who feel they have been unfairly or inaccurately rated?

970. What kinds of performance factors / elements do you use?

971. What is a general description of the processes under performance measurement and assessment?

972. How should adaptive assessments be implemented?

973. Is it critical or vital to the job?

974. To what degree do team members articulate the teams work approach?

975. How do you currently use the time that is

available?

976. Are the draft goals SMART ?

977. New skills/knowledge gained this year?

978. To what degree are the goals ambitious?

979. What is collaboration?

980. What are the standards or expectations for success?

981. What are the key duties or tasks of the Ratee?

982. How will you identify your Team Leaders?

983. Who they are?

3.10 Issue Log: Competitive Threats

984. Who were proponents/opponents?

985. Is the issue log kept in a safe place?

986. What is the stakeholders political influence?

987. Who are the members of the governing body?

988. In classifying stakeholders, which approach to do so are you using?

989. Are there too many who have an interest in some aspect of your work?

990. In your work, how much time is spent on stakeholder identification?

991. What is a Stakeholder?

992. Are the stakeholders getting the information they need, are they consulted, are concerns addressed?

993. How often do you engage with stakeholders?

994. Can an impact cause deviation beyond team, stage or Competitive Threats project tolerances?

995. Who reported the issue?

996. What would have to change?

997. Are they needed?

998. What is the status of the issue?

4.0 Monitoring and Controlling Process Group: Competitive Threats

999. Have operating capacities been created and/or reinforced in partners?

1000. How to ensure validity, quality and consistency?

1001. How is agile portfolio management done?

1002. How can you make your needs known?

1003. What is the expected monetary value of the Competitive Threats project?

1004. Is it what was agreed upon?

1005. Did you implement the program as designed?

1006. Based on your Competitive Threats project communication management plan, what worked well?

1007. If a risk event occurs, what will you do?

1008. What resources are necessary?

1009. What communication items need improvement?

1010. Is the verbiage used appropriate and understandable?

1011. How well did the team follow the chosen processes?

1012. Purpose: toward what end is the evaluation being conducted?

1013. What is the timeline?

1014. Are there areas that need improvement?

1015. How will staff learn how to use the deliverables?

1016. Accuracy: what design will lead to accurate information?

1017. How is agile Competitive Threats project management done?

4.1 Project Performance Report: Competitive Threats

1018. To what degree does the informal organization make use of individual resources and meet individual needs?

1019. To what degree are the demands of the task compatible with and converge with the relationships of the informal organization?

1020. To what degree will each member have the opportunity to advance his or her professional skills in all three of the above categories while contributing to the accomplishment of the teams purpose and goals?

1021. To what degree does the funding match the requirement?

1022. To what degree does the teams work approach provide opportunity for members to engage in open interaction?

1023. To what degree are sub-teams possible or necessary?

1024. What is the degree to which rules govern information exchange between groups?

1025. To what degree do the relationships of the informal organization motivate taskrelevant behavior and facilitate task completion?

1026. To what degree will the team adopt a concrete, clearly understood, and agreed-upon approach that will result in achievement of the teams goals?

1027. To what degree do team members understand one anothers roles and skills?

1028. To what degree will the team ensure that all members equitably share the work essential to the success of the team?

1029. To what degree does the teams purpose contain themes that are particularly meaningful and memorable?

1030. To what degree does the teams work approach provide opportunity for members to engage in fact-based problem solving?

1031. To what degree do the structures of the formal organization motivate taskrelevant behavior and facilitate task completion?

1032. To what degree can team members meet frequently enough to accomplish the teams ends?

1033. To what degree does the task meet individual needs?

4.2 Variance Analysis: Competitive Threats

1034. What business event causes fluctuations?

1035. Did a new competitor enter the market?

1036. Are the wbs and organizational levels for application of the Competitive Threats projected overhead costs identified?

1037. How are variances affected by multiple material and labor categories?

1038. Can process improvements lead to unfavorable variances?

1039. Favorable or unfavorable variance?

1040. What does an unfavorable overhead volume variance mean?

1041. Do the rates and prices remain constant throughout the year?

1042. What does a favorable labor efficiency variance mean?

1043. Who are responsible for overhead performance control of related costs?

1044. What are the direct labor dollars and/or hours?

1045. How does your organization measure performance?

1046. Why are standard cost systems used?

1047. Are estimates of costs at completion generated in a rational, consistent manner?

1048. Is there a logical explanation for any variance?

1049. How does your organization allocate the cost of shared expenses and services?

1050. Are work packages assigned to performing organizations?

4.3 Earned Value Status: Competitive Threats

1051. Validation is a process of ensuring that the developed system will actually achieve the stakeholders desired outcomes; Are you building the right product? What do you validate?

1052. Are you hitting your Competitive Threats projects targets?

1053. Verification is a process of ensuring that the developed system satisfies the stakeholders agreements and specifications; Are you building the product right? What do you verify?

1054. Where is evidence-based earned value in your organization reported?

1055. How much is it going to cost by the finish?

1056. Where are your problem areas?

1057. What is the unit of forecast value?

1058. When is it going to finish?

1059. If earned value management (EVM) is so good in determining the true status of a Competitive Threats project and Competitive Threats project its completion, why is it that hardly any one uses it in information systems related Competitive Threats projects?

1060. How does this compare with other Competitive Threats projects?

1061. Earned value can be used in almost any Competitive Threats project situation and in almost any Competitive Threats project environment. it may be used on large Competitive Threats projects, medium sized Competitive Threats projects, tiny Competitive Threats projects (in cut-down form), complex and simple Competitive Threats projects and in any market sector. some people, of course, know all about earned value, they have used it for years - but perhaps not as effectively as they could have?

4.4 Risk Audit: Competitive Threats

1062. Are procedures in place to ensure the security of staff and information and compliance with privacy legislation if applicable?

1063. What are the outcomes you are looking for?

1064. Who is responsible for what?

1065. Can assurance be expanded beyond the traditional audit without undermining independence?

1066. What does your data tell you about your risks?

1067. Do the people have the right combinations of skills?

1068. Are there any forms the staff is required to sign?

1069. What programmatic and Fiscal information is being collected and analyzed?

1070. How risk averse are you?

1071. Are end-users enthusiastically committed to the Competitive Threats project and the system/product to be built?

1072. Does your organization have a register of insurance policies detailing all current insurance policies?

1073. Are all financial transactions accurately recorded

(receipted, banked)?

1074. What can you do to manage outcomes?

1075. If applicable; which route/packaging option do you choose for transport of hazmat material?

1076. How are risk appetites expressed?

1077. Have all involved been advised of any obligations they have to sponsors?

1078. Is the customer willing to establish rapid communication links with the developer?

1079. Does the adoption of a business risk audit approach change internal control documentation and testing practices?

1080. Does the implementation method matter?

4.5 Contractor Status Report: Competitive Threats

1081. How long have you been using the services?

1082. How is risk transferred?

1083. What is the average response time for answering a support call?

1084. Describe how often regular updates are made to the proposed solution. Are corresponding regular updates included in the standard maintenance plan?

1085. Are there contractual transfer concerns?

1086. What was the budget or estimated cost for your organizations services?

1087. What process manages the contracts?

1088. If applicable; describe your standard schedule for new software version releases. Are new software version releases included in the standard maintenance plan?

1089. What was the actual budget or estimated cost for your organizations services?

1090. Who can list a Competitive Threats project as organization experience, your organization or a previous employee of your organization?

1091. What was the overall budget or estimated cost?

1092. What are the minimum and optimal bandwidth requirements for the proposed solution?

1093. What was the final actual cost?

4.6 Formal Acceptance: Competitive Threats

1094. What are the requirements against which to test, Who will execute?

1095. How does your team plan to obtain formal acceptance on your Competitive Threats project?

1096. What lessons were learned about your Competitive Threats project management methodology?

1097. General estimate of the costs and times to complete the Competitive Threats project?

1098. Was the sponsor/customer satisfied?

1099. How well did the team follow the methodology?

1100. What was done right?

1101. Do you perform formal acceptance or burn-in tests?

1102. What features, practices, and processes proved to be strengths or weaknesses?

1103. What can you do better next time?

1104. What function(s) does it fill or meet?

1105. Was the Competitive Threats project work

done on time, within budget, and according to specification?

1106. Do you buy pre-configured systems or build your own configuration?

1107. What is the Acceptance Management Process?

1108. Who supplies data?

1109. Was business value realized?

1110. Does it do what Competitive Threats project team said it would?

1111. Do you buy-in installation services?

1112. Who would use it?

1113. Did the Competitive Threats project manager and team act in a professional and ethical manner?

5.0 Closing Process Group: Competitive Threats

1114. Is this a follow-on to a previous Competitive Threats project?

1115. How will you know you did it?

1116. Did the Competitive Threats project management methodology work?

1117. What were things that you did well, and could improve, and how?

1118. How well defined and documented were the Competitive Threats project management processes you chose to use?

1119. Are there funding or time constraints?

1120. What is an Encumbrance?

1121. Contingency planning. if a risk event occurs, what will you do?

1122. What level of risk does the proposed budget represent to the Competitive Threats project?

1123. What is the Competitive Threats project Management Process?

1124. Just how important is your work to the overall success of the Competitive Threats project?

1125. Were cost budgets met?

1126. How well did the chosen processes fit the needs of the Competitive Threats project?

1127. How well did you do?

1128. What areas were overlooked on this Competitive Threats project?

5.1 Procurement Audit: Competitive Threats

1129. Was the overall procurement done within a reasonable time?

1130. Does the strategy discus the best manner of purchase, considering the types of goods and services needed?

1131. Has the expected benefits from realisation of the procurement Competitive Threats project been calculated?

1132. Was the award decision based on the result of the evaluation of tenders?

1133. Are transportation charges verified?

1134. Is there a formal program of inservice training for personnel in the business management function?

1135. Was additional significant information supplied to all interested parties?

1136. Has your organization clearly defined the award criteria?

1137. Have guidelines been set up for how the procurement process should be conducted?

1138. Could bidders learn all relevant information straight from the tender documents?

1139. Are individuals with check-signing responsibility prohibited from signing blank checks?

1140. Were additional deliveries a partial replacement for normal supplies or installations or an extension of existing supplies or installations?

1141. Did the contracting authority offer unrestricted and full electronic access to the contract documents and any supplementary documents (specifying the internet address in the notice)?

1142. Is there a procedure on requesting bids?

1143. Are all purchase orders cancelled after payment to avoid duplicate payment of the same invoice?

1144. Do appropriate controls ensure that procurement decisions are not biased by conflicts of interest or corruption?

1145. Are staff members evaluated in accordance with the terms of existing negotiated agreements?

1146. Is your organization aware and informed about international procurement standards and good practice?

1147. Has your organization procedures in place to monitor the input of experts employed to assist the procurement function?

1148. Are there performance targets on value for money obtained and cost savings?

5.2 Contract Close-Out: Competitive Threats

1149. Parties: Authorized?

1150. Parties: who is involved?

1151. Change in knowledge?

1152. How is the contracting office notified of the automatic contract close-out?

1153. Have all contract records been included in the Competitive Threats project archives?

1154. How does it work?

1155. Change in attitude or behavior?

1156. How/when used ?

1157. Was the contract type appropriate?

1158. Has each contract been audited to verify acceptance and delivery?

1159. Was the contract complete without requiring numerous changes and revisions?

1160. Are the signers the authorized officials?

1161. Have all contracts been completed?

1162. Change in circumstances?

1163. What happens to the recipient of services?

1164. What is capture management?

1165. Have all acceptance criteria been met prior to final payment to contractors?

1166. Was the contract sufficiently clear so as not to result in numerous disputes and misunderstandings?

1167. Have all contracts been closed?

5.3 Project or Phase Close-Out: Competitive Threats

1168. How often did each stakeholder need an update?

1169. What was the preferred delivery mechanism?

1170. When and how were information needs best met?

1171. What is the information level of detail required for each stakeholder?

1172. What is a Risk Management Process?

1173. If you were the Competitive Threats project sponsor, how would you determine which Competitive Threats project team(s) and/or individuals deserve recognition?

1174. Is the lesson significant, valid, and applicable?

1175. What could have been improved?

1176. Planned completion date?

1177. Who controlled key decisions that were made?

1178. Who is responsible for award close-out?

1179. What are the marketing communication needs for each stakeholder?

1180. Were the outcomes different from the already stated planned?

1181. What are the mandatory communication needs for each stakeholder?

1182. Who controlled the resources for the Competitive Threats project?

1183. What information is each stakeholder group interested in?

1184. Does the lesson educate others to improve performance?

1185. What are they?

1186. In preparing the Lessons Learned report, should it reflect a consensus viewpoint, or should the report reflect the different individual viewpoints?

1187. What information did each stakeholder need to contribute to the Competitive Threats projects success?

5.4 Lessons Learned: Competitive Threats

1188. If issue escalation was required, how effectively were issues resolved?

1189. How effective was the acceptance management process?

1190. What is the growth stage of the organization?

1191. How effectively were issues managed on the Competitive Threats project?

1192. How useful was the content of the training you received in preparation for the use of the product/service?

1193. For the next Competitive Threats project, how could you improve on the way Competitive Threats project was conducted?

1194. What would you like to see better documented about how to use existing processes on this type of Competitive Threats project?

1195. What surprises did the team have to deal with?

1196. How effective was the documentation that you received with the Competitive Threats project product/service?

1197. What is the growth stage of your organization?

1198. How efficient and effective were Competitive Threats project team meetings?

1199. How much of your time was spent on other than this Competitive Threats project?

1200. What did you put in place to ensure success?

1201. What were the most significant issues on this Competitive Threats project?

1202. Who had fiscal authority to manage the funding for the Competitive Threats project, did that work?

1203. Where do you go from here?

1204. Overall, how effective was the performance of the Competitive Threats project Manager?

1205. What are the influence patterns?

1206. What were the major enablers to a quick response?

1207. What is the desired end-state?

Index

277

identified   1, 16-17, 21, 32, 39, 58, 62, 64, 72, 84-85, 147, 151,
153-154, 173, 183, 187, 190, 199, 203, 212, 227, 240
identify9-10, 19, 24, 58, 64, 69, 145, 168, 178, 182, 208, 223, 233
ignore 21
ignoring   103
imbedded   92
immediate   131, 197
impact4, 28, 46, 48, 51-53, 55, 80, 121, 126, 139, 142, 173, 180,
195, 197-199, 201, 220, 227, 234
impacted   53, 126, 146
impacts   46, 50, 169
implement   15, 51, 66, 88, 236
implicit 121
importance 230
important   21, 31, 63, 68, 71, 103, 114, 118, 120, 128, 165,
207, 228, 230-231, 250
improve   2, 9, 64, 73-74, 76-77, 79-82, 84, 165, 183-184, 226,
250, 257-258
improved   79, 82, 85, 87, 90, 208, 256
improves   127
improving   83, 216
incentives 93
incident   197, 221
include   16, 74, 85, 154, 157, 207, 231
included   2, 7, 23, 47, 142, 170, 175, 177, 217-218, 246, 254
INCLUDES   9
including   16, 32-33, 39, 46, 51, 71, 95-96, 98, 147, 152, 210
increase   75, 119
increased   101
increasing 116
incurred   53
incurring   152
in-depth   8, 10
indicate   62, 94, 116
indicated   96
indicators 21, 47, 52, 63, 68, 70, 79, 95, 196
indirect   47, 152, 175, 187
indirectly 1
individual 1, 47, 134, 156, 190, 192, 230, 238-239, 257
inducting   224
industry   93, 117, 119, 154, 224
infinite 107
influence   77, 118, 130, 193-194, 222, 234, 259

problem   15, 19-25, 27, 30, 39-41, 52-53, 68, 70, 131, 139, 141, 215, 222, 239, 242
problems   19, 21-24, 84, 87, 96, 119, 142, 186
procedure   154, 223-224, 253
procedures   9, 79, 90-91, 95, 98, 137, 148, 151, 164, 172, 179, 182, 209-210, 244, 253
proceed   187, 199
process   1-7, 9, 27-29, 31, 35, 38, 40, 45, 58-64, 67-72, 74, 89-90, 92-99, 126-127, 133, 136-137, 142-143, 145-147, 154, 164, 168-169, 182, 185-186, 196, 209, 213-214, 226-227, 230, 236, 240, 242, 246, 249-250, 252, 256, 258
processes   48, 55, 59, 63-67, 69, 71-72, 93, 96, 127, 131, 133, 137, 145, 147, 151, 167, 174, 195, 201, 210, 213, 219, 223, 232, 237, 248, 250-251, 258
procuring   152
produce   66, 164, 213, 215
produced   72, 78
producing   143
product   1, 43, 63, 68, 105, 111, 133, 137, 139, 145-146, 161, 179-180, 182, 184, 200, 203, 215, 226, 242, 244, 258
production   32, 76, 101
products   1, 24, 26, 51, 114, 129, 134, 143, 175, 184, 200, 216, 219
profile 197
profits 180
program   26, 47, 60, 89, 127, 132, 190, 198, 214, 236, 252
programs   193, 215, 223
progress   36, 50, 76, 98, 102, 110, 134, 155, 178, 182, 185, 205, 209-210, 213, 231
prohibited   151, 253
project 2-4, 6-8, 16, 19, 23, 33, 64-65, 88, 99, 101-102, 106-108, 112, 114-115, 120, 122, 125-131, 133-139, 141-143, 145-147, 149-150, 154-163, 165, 167-178, 180-182, 187, 189-193, 195, 197-199, 201-202, 205-206, 209-211, 213-216, 219, 227, 234, 236-238, 242-244, 246, 248-252, 254, 256-259
projected   153, 180, 240
projects   2, 106, 112, 125, 127, 133, 143, 146, 148, 150, 167-168, 171, 179, 189, 193, 200, 202, 215-216, 242-243, 257
promising   111
promote   51, 57
promptly   176
proofing   74
proper 94, 137, 139, 153, 187

suppliers   27, 68, 102, 224
supplies   249, 253
supply 45, 160, 211
support   7, 20, 68, 88, 90, 96, 106, 114, 116, 142, 164, 188-189, 212, 222, 224, 246
supported   65, 224
supporting   77, 94, 137, 185
supportive   189
supports   127
surface   96
surprises   258
SUSTAIN   2, 77, 100
sustaining   95
symptom   15, 54
system 9, 31, 61, 70, 96, 102, 123, 139, 141-142, 148, 152, 218, 220, 222, 224-225, 242, 244
systematic   48
systems   64, 69, 71-72, 76-77, 93, 131, 148, 168, 173, 224, 241-242, 249
tackle 54
tactics 222
taking 127, 215
talent 67, 117
talents 116
talking 7
tangle 187
target 34, 103, 154
targets 104, 131, 242, 253
tasked 93
teaching   224
teamed   228
teaming   228-229
technical   85, 141, 147, 167, 207
techniques   58, 102, 126, 138, 155, 174
technology   52, 93, 111, 128, 161, 167-168, 199, 228-229
templates   7-8
tender 252
tenders   252
testable   38
test-cycle   185
tested 20
testing 184, 195, 209, 245
thematic   131

301

CPSIA information can be obtained
at www.ICGtesting.com
Printed in the USA
BVHW082020110819
555624BV00016BA/1794/P

9 780655 840244